Ghosts of Ottawa

From the files of the Haunted Walk

Ghosts of Ottawa

From the files of the Haunted Walk

Glen Shackleton
Haunted Walks Inc.
Ottawa

North America & international
toll-free: 844-688-6899 (USA & Canada)
fax: 812 355 4082

Contributors

Glen Shackleton
Jim Dean
Dominique Lajoie
Stephanie Robinson
Margo MacDonald
Annie Lachance
Kristina Lillico

Cover Art

Richard Lawley

Photography

Katie Refling

Table of Contents

This book is dedicated to the many amazing tour guides who have brought Ottawa's haunted history to life for over a decade.

I also thank my parents.
Without their support the Haunted Walk could never have begun.

Preface

It did not take long for me to become comfortable with the idea that Ottawa was a very haunted city. In that first year of conducting Haunted Walk tours, initially in Kingston, Ontario, it was not at all unusual for one of our customers from the Ottawa area to comment that they knew plenty of well-known haunted spots in the nation's capital that we should really investigate. As a regular visitor and sometime-resident of Ottawa for most of my school-age years, I knew it had potential.

At first glance, Ottawa may seem like a strange place for a ghost tour. It is perhaps better-known for its role as the home of our politicians and national institutions than for any sort of "darker history". It did not take much investigation to realize that our true history was very different from that conveyed by our staid and quiet reputation. In its early days, old Bytown, as the community was originally named, had a reputation as one of the most dangerous towns in North America. It was a place filled with lumbermen, brothels and regular violence in the streets. It came as quite a shock to Canadians when it was named as the new capital of a united Canada in 1857. Though there were very good reasons for the choice, it was very difficult to see past the rough-and-tumble reality of the place at the time.

It was clear enough that Ottawa was a place with an

interesting history, but what about the ghosts? I was aware of some of the more famous haunted spots, such as the Museum of Nature or the old Carleton County Jail, which has a worldwide reputation as a destination of choice for ghost hunters, but what about the lesser-known stories? After asking a lot of questions of some very helpful people, and conducting many months of research, I was delighted to find that Ottawa had its own rich history of ghost stories. All the necessary pieces were falling into place for the creation of the first Haunted Walk of Ottawa.

Our Ottawa tours began in 1996, with regular evening walks departing from the grounds of the Ottawa Jail Hostel. For the first few seasons, our tours concentrated on the neighbourhood of Sandy Hill. As our collection of downtown ghost stories became too compelling to resist, we moved to our new start location at the corner of Sparks and Elgin, not far from the site of one of the most famous murders in Canadian history.

As on our Kingston tours, it was not always easy to explain to people what exactly it was we were doing, dressed in cloaks and carrying lanterns, walking around the city at night. On more than one occasion, concerned citizens were quick to contact the authorities to report that a "cult" had been seen in their neighbourhood. Today, after many years of conducting tours, we are happy to say that most Ottawans consider the Haunted Walk to be an iconic local event, and one which expresses an important side of the character of our city.

What has perhaps distinguished our tours of Ottawa most of all is that many of our staff and customers have had a chance to share in these experiences for themselves. We have been blessed with the opportunity, over the years, to explore a number of haunted buildings, spend the night on death row at the old jail, and experience many of these ghostly encounters for ourselves.

This added immensely to our understanding of these places, and of the spooky and perhaps supernatural happenings for which they are famous.

In this collection of our favourite stories, we are hoping to share not only some of the most famous and well-loved ghost stories of the nation's capital, but also some of our own personal accounts of the supernatural. We hope that you enjoy reading our stories every bit as much as we have enjoyed collecting and sharing them.

Glen Shackleton, founder of Haunted Walks Inc.

What are ghosts anyway?
by Glen Shackleton, Director
Haunted Walks Inc.

One could easily be excused for assuming that after more than a decade of searching for evidence of the supernatural, I must have a decisive answer to this question. I have certainly spent enough time thinking and talking about ghosts to know that the issue is not as simple as it might at first appear.

The first thing we must ask ourselves is what, specifically, we mean by "ghosts." Many of the stories we have come across certainly seem to involve supernatural events or, at the very least, events that are difficult if not impossible to explain, but ghost stories come in many different forms. When we refer to ghosts, do we mean, for example, a physical manifestation of a dead person's image, a strong sense of a presence in a building, the phenomenon of objects moving without explanation, or even just a strong sense that someone we know has died? Tales of these very different phenomena are generally considered to be "ghost stories," but do they all have the same root cause, and are they all signs of the same type of paranormal activity?

The classic ghost that first comes to mind usually takes the form of a faded image or a sense of someone or something that existed in the past. A building that was occupied for many years by a strong personality, or that perhaps was the scene of tragic events, may well seem to hold onto an impression of its past. These types of encounters seldom seem to involve an "intelligent" spirit, or at least not one that seems to have the ability to interact with our world. Those who experience this type of encounter usually describe it as though they were seeing a past event play out, an event that may have repeated itself many times before. An example of this type of encounter would be a number of different witnesses seeing the image of a woman walking up and down the stairs at the same time every night. Are they truly seeing a ghost, or is this a reflection of some human ability to see events that transpired in the past? Perhaps we see these events with something like peripheral vision; we have some ability to sense them, but only in fleeting and unclear glimpses.

Some ghosts seem to manifest themselves in the physical world. Objects move or are thrown about a room, fires start without explanation, doors slam shut or footsteps are heard from otherwise calm and empty rooms. These encounters are rarely harmful, but are always frightening. It has been suggested that these "poltergeist" encounters may be a sign of some psychic abilities among the living people who are present when they occur, but most of the incidents that we have come across seem to have a more ghostly cause.

The most terrifying experiences are also the most uncommon. These are encounters with a seemingly intelligent presence, one that interacts with the living and our world. These spirits do not always come across as malevolent, and sometimes fall under the category of "friendly ghosts." They seem to represent the spirit of a person who was once alive, and have just as many different personalities as there are types of people – kind or cruel, helpful or harmful. My own experience is that most people who relate a story of a home that is haunted in this manner have learned to get along with their ghosts, almost as though they were members of the family. The people lose their fear once they realize that no harm is intended. Others are not so fortunate, and have experiences that most of us are grateful not to share.

The examples I have mentioned are only the most common types of ghostly encounters, but we can add to this list experiences of ghost ships and ghost animals, premonitions, and many others. There are so many different types of unexplained and ghostly encounters that it is easy to see how difficult it is to find one explanation that fits all of them. If it is impossible to explain ghosts in any simple way, is there anything we can do to find out more about them? Is there any way to prove that ghosts exist?

In recent years there has been a huge increase in the popularity of ghost investigations, and many attempts have been made to find scientific proof of the existence of ghosts. Dozens of television shows and paranormal investigation clubs have sprung up, ranging from the insightful to the ridiculous. Many people make use of scientific instruments to try to find changes in temperature or magnetic fields in haunted spots, or attempt to capture ghostly activity through photographs or recorded sounds. Others, like me, who consider themselves ghost historians, also believe that an investigation into the history of a building can provide important clues as to the possible reasons for a haunting. This focus on gathering scientific evidence has proven very valuable to understanding purported haunted sites, but it does have its limits. Critical questions are not always asked about what exactly the ghost investigator believes is being measured. A photograph filled with glowing "orbs" can often be easily explained by the presence of dust or moisture in the air, yet many internet sites would have you believe that these are indisputable proof of a gateway to another dimension. Electro-magnetic field (EMF) disruptions can most logically be tied to causes that are not supernatural. Electronic equipment and plumbing have both been known to cause EMF detectors to give false readings. In any case, where is the proof that the spirit of a dead person can cause changes in these fields? A ghost investigator must be vigilant to ensure that the gathering of large amounts of raw data does not completely replace the logical process of deduction.

This is not to say that the true skeptics are any less guilty of making too many assumptions, as they often will go to any lengths to attempt to debunk an account of paranormal activity, no matter what the evidence in its favour. It is important to take a critical look at unusual claims; simple explanations can often be found, but there are also many situations we have investigated which seem to have no easy explanation. A ghost story appears most convincing when there are a variety of types of evidence involved, as well as more than one witness. In general, I see ghost investigation as the process of amassing circumstantial evidence. The goal is not so much to prove the existence of ghosts as it is to add new information to a wonderful mystery that we may never understand.

The one thing that everyone can agree on is that ghost stories are likely to continue to fascinate us. Every culture has its own traditions of ghost stories and the supernatural. There are as many different beliefs about ghosts as there are stories, and it is possible that we may have to accept that the question "What are ghosts?" is one to which there will never be a definitive answer.

The Bytown Museum at the Rideau Canal

The Bytown Museum
A Personal Account by Glen Shackleton

As the Director of Haunted Walks Inc., I am often asked if I have ever encountered one of our ghosts for myself. My experience at the Bytown Museum was certainly one of the most frightening moments of my life. After many years of volunteering at the building, I have perhaps gotten over this initial shock, and have come to regard it as a building filled with character and charm. While I still love to visit the exhibits on the history of early Ottawa, I admit I will seldom do so on my own!

When I first heard of the haunted Bytown Museum, I must admit I was a little skeptical. I was aware that the museum, a looming stone edifice of three stories that housed all sorts of strange and sometimes creepy artifacts from the early history of the city was the oldest stone building in Ottawa. It struck me that many of the "supernatural encounters" which had occurred there were of the type that could be nothing more than the product of an overactive imagination paired with a unique and spooky location. This turned out to be a rather hasty judgment.

The building was officially called the Commissariat, and was built in 1827 to house military supplies and money needed for the construction of the Rideau Canal that runs from Ottawa to Kingston. It is now a museum which commemorates the construction of the canal and life in old Bytown. It is a fantastic museum with which I have now been involved for many years as a volunteer, but it also has the reputation of being one of Ottawa's most haunted buildings.

Perhaps the most common experience described by visitors to the museum is the sound of heavy footsteps behind them on the stairs. When they stop and turn around, no-one is there, but the footsteps continue on for a step or two. I personally always believed this to be a ghost story with a simple explanation. I reasoned that if the old wood on the stairs became compressed when a visitor stepped on it, it might make a noise like a footstep when it sprang back into shape. In 2006 I had an experience that most definitely changed my opinion. I was walking up the stairs from the gift shop while talking to Steve, the museum's Program Coordinator, who I was certain was following right behind me. I turned to ask him a question when I realized that he was no longer there and had gone back downstairs to get something. I distinctly heard the footsteps follow me for a step or two, just as had been described by many witnesses before. I also had the very strong sensation of a presence there with me on the stairs. I can only say that it was a very convincing personal experience. The sound of the footsteps was too distinct, and the feeling that someone else was there was simply too strong for me to discount it as easily as I had in the past.

The staff and researchers who work at the Bytown Museum have long been convinced that the building is haunted. Often the motion detectors set off the alarms when the building is closed at night, with no explanation. One interpreter who worked there for five years felt that she got to know the ghost quite well, and he often enjoyed playing tricks on her. One of his favourite tricks was to turn historical videos on and off when no one was in the room.

He especially liked the "Log Drivers' Waltz". One particular time when she was working in the next room, she heard it come on and was so frustrated that she yelled out: "Stop that! You know I hate that song!" Immediately, it stopped.

It may be for this reason that the ghost became known as "Duncan", in honour of one of the first storekeepers at the Commissariat, a man named Duncan Macnab. He had a reputation as a bit of a trickster. Rum and supplies often seemed to disappear while under his care. More than once he was called upon to come up with explanations for these missing supplies to the Commissary General in Quebec, his supervisor at the time. On one occasion, when a large amount of rum went missing, he explained that it had "evaporated", even though it was the middle of winter at the time. The records also show that a man who died while Macnab was in charge continued to receive full rations for a week after his death, and Macnab offered no explanation as to what had become of these rations. Macnab enjoyed playing tricks on people so much during his lifetime that he may still be playing tricks on people in the building to this day.

In August of 2000 I had my most frightening personal experience at the Bytown Museum. One evening I had scheduled a staff event at the museum. The plan was that we would have a brief staff meeting and then watch the movie The Sixth Sense at the museum. In the end, it turned out I was the only one who hadn't either seen the movie or had the ending spoiled for them by a friend. We decided to stop for a pint at D'Arcy McGee's Irish Pub and held our meeting there instead. At the end of the meeting I realized that I had not set the alarm in the museum, and as it was dark and late, I asked for some volunteers to join me. Two tour guides, Margo and Emily, joined me, along with Emily's mother, who was visiting from out of town.

Since we had a visitor with us, we decided to show her one of the stranger artifacts in the museum; the death hand of D'Arcy McGee. The Victorians had a particular penchant for making plaster casts of the faces of famous people who had died. Since this was impossible in the case of D'Arcy McGee (as he had been shot in the head), a cast was made of his hand instead. As it has always been one of my favourite museum displays, we decided to head up to the third floor for a look.

We took a quick look around the third floor, then Margo and I wandered down to the second floor, leaving Emily and her mother to have a final look at the displays before we left for the night. Standing around the corner from the main staircase leading down to the gift shop below, we were very unnerved to hear footsteps coming up the stairs. It was such a clear sound that we both gave each other that look that says, "Are you hearing what I'm hearing?" We peeked carefully around the corner. As we feared (and suspected), no one was there. My immediate thought was that it could be an echo caused by our companions moving around on the floor above. We checked and found that Emily and her mother were still standing in front of the same display where we last saw them. They hadn't moved a step from their position at the top of the stairs. At this point we decided it was time to leave.

The four of us descended to the gift shop level and began the process of closing the building. I crossed the gift shop to the alarm panel while my three companions waited by the main entrance to the building. I was chatting with the three of them across the room as I put down my briefcase, and closed the wooden sliding door that separated the gift-shop from the rest of the building. I pointed out the security display behind the counter

Main stairs leading up from the gift shop.

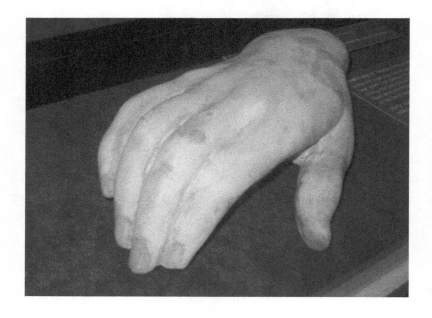

The Death Hand of Thomas D'Arcy McGee

and made a joke that if anyone appeared on camera in the room on the other side of the sliding door, I was "out of there". I was standing there, trying to remember the code to activate the alarm, when the shaking started. The sliding door began to swing and shake, slowly at first, and then more and more violently. It was just as if there were someone on the other side of the door, trying to get out. Some of the souvenirs on the shelf were rattling away and the door was swinging noticeably back and forth noticeably less than a foot away from my face.

Before this happened to me, I had long wondered what my reaction would be if I were put in a truly terrifying situation. I liked to think that I would be more likely to have the animal instinct of "fight" rather than "flight". When faced with this situation, all I could conjure up in the way of animal instincts was that of a deer caught in the headlights. I stood there, frozen in fear, staring at this happening in front of me. The most courage I could muster was to turn to the other three and say "Uh...guys, did you see that?" As I turned, I caught sight of the other three running out the front doors of the building.

After a moment, Margo, in a moment of exquisite bravery, came back into the gift shop and led me out the front door. The four of us stood there in the parking lot in a state of both panic and wonder. After we all calmed down a little they were able to tell me that they had not seen the door shaking at all. Instead, all three had been terrified to hear the sound of heavy footsteps, as though made by heavy boots, walking across the ceiling and heading in their direction. They were all absolutely convinced of what they had heard, and they were able to describe in detail the exact sound and rhythm that the footsteps had made.

We got up the nerve to re-enter the building, set the alarm

and grab the gear I had left behind. We waited in the parking lot for a full thirty minutes, almost hoping to hear the alarm go off. We were so convinced that someone had to be in the building with us, playing a prank, that we thought about calling the police to teach them a lesson. After thirty minutes had passed, the motion detectors and alarms had not been activated and it was clear there was no one else in the building.

When I arrived home that night and crawled into bed, my wife woke up and asked me why I had left my bedside light on. I assured her she didn't want to know.

Watson's Mill in Manotick

Watson's Mill

Just below Parliament Hill lies the Ottawa River. Not far to the east is the spot where it meets the Rideau River, which in 1827 became a central part of the Rideau Canal waterway. This junction is the biggest reason for the settlement of the Ottawa area, with the rivers providing transportation, and later, a source of power. Mills of different kinds were often the centre of these new communities, and many have their own ghost stories.

The grist mill in the village of Manotick, just outside Ottawa, is no exception. The mill was built and owned by Moss Dickenson, the town founder, and his partner, Joseph Currier. Both men were very prominent figures in local history. Moss Dickenson had grown wealthy in the shipping business and owned a fleet of 16 steamships and 60 barges that would transport livestock, grain, lumber and passengers back and forth between Kingston and Ottawa. In 1859, he partnered with Joseph Currier to build a local mill. Currier had experience at running sawmills in Buckingham and New Edinburgh before commencing business on his own account. By the time he worked with Dickenson on the Manotick project, he was quite a wealthy and important local businessman. He would later go on to become a prominent politician and the owner of several important businesses. He became the president of the Ottawa Citizen newspaper and the

Gatineau Valley Railway Company. He built several homes, including one which would later become 24 Sussex Drive, the home of Canada's Prime Minister. Sadly for Currier, much of this success in life was preceded by a terrible accident.

In 1861 Courier married 20-year-old Ann Crosby from Lake George, New York. One month after the wedding, in the month of January, he brought his new wife to see the mill for the first time. The occasion was a celebration to commemorate the first anniversary of the opening of the mill. Currier began to talk business with Dickenson and others, while Ann decided to explore the mill on her own. Unfortunately, while she was on the second floor of the building her dress got caught in a revolving turbine shaft. Some locals will tell you that she was sucked into the mill and was ground up in the machine, but the truth wasn't nearly so gruesome, though no less tragic. She was thrown into one of the support pillars nearby and hit her head on a beam, which killed her instantly. Her husband was understandably devastated. He sold his shares in the business and left Manotick for good. Much of his later success was attributed to the hard work he put in as a means to forget this terrible loss.

Ever since that tragic day, the mill has been said to be haunted. It is run as a local museum, and dozens of visitors and staff members say they have heard footsteps and wailing noises, or seen strange things happen in the mill. Many visitors say they will feel an unexplained cold patch in an otherwise warm building. Some even claim that they have seen the image of Ann herself in the mill, when the building is closed, moving from window to window and watching over her husband's business to this day. She is often described as a beautiful, tall, flaxen-haired woman who will peer out of the windows on the second floor.

In 2007 a group of Haunted Walk tour guides led by our

Ghost Investigation Unit decided to conduct an informal ghost investigation and spend the night at Watson's Mill. It was not meant to be a scientific investigation, but we did our best to take the job seriously. We started by covering up the descriptive panels that referred to the story of Ann Currier, and the haunting at the museum, as we did not want to bias the majority of investigators who had never been to the site and had no prior knowledge of the history of the place. At one point in the night, groups of investigators were sent into the building to see if they could pick up any vibes, or perhaps witness the haunting themselves. They entered two at a time, and explored the spooky old wooden building, with only the glow of a flashlight, and the dull roar of the river moving underneath and next to the building to keep them company. Most experienced nothing of note, other than the odd sense of a presence, or other feelings easily attributed to the atmosphere of the place.

One pair of investigators had a far more convincing experience. They had explored the first and second floors without incident and were about to ascend the wooden steps into the dark attic above, but they both froze in their tracks at the same moment and looked at each other. Both investigators had distinctly heard the sound of male voices above them, directly at the top of the stairs. Though they could not make out the words, it sounded as though someone did not want their company. In their opinion, it was far too distinctly located within the building to have been caused by distant traffic or another outside noise. The rest of the team waiting outside later confirmed there had been no such noises at the time of the incident.

The first thought on both of their minds was that it had been a cruel prank, played by one of the other investigators or a member of the museum staff. It seemed far too distinct and obvious to be a legitimate supernatural experience. With some help from a handful of brave volunteers, a thorough search revealed nothing hidden in the attic. Some suggestions were made to explain the noise, such as distant traffic passing over a bridge, but none that could convince the two who had actually heard the voices that night. They were both left feeling quite shaken up by the experience.

A little later in the evening, as the investigators gathered together to discuss the evening's events, the story of Ann Currier was revealed to the group. Several members of the group were already familiar with this part of the story. An aspect of the story that no one had heard was revealed when the museum displays were uncovered. Among the accounts of frightening encounters in the building was an explanation that many visitors and staff had heard "angry male voices coming from the area of the attic". It was a reference that some members of our group were not terribly pleased to see, and many of the investigators slept poorly that night.

The Highway Ghost
A Personal Account by Annie (tour guide)

Annie was a tour guide who worked for the Haunted Walk for several years. She was always a favourite of our French customers, and well loved by her co-workers. Little did they know that she had her very own true and very tragic ghost story. When listening to Annie tell her tale, it was impossible not to be affected by it, and she seldom left a dry eye in any crowd who was lucky enough to hear her tell it.

I come from the Saguenay-Lac-Saint-Jean region in Quebec. The first time I left home was to study law at Laval University. Even if Quebec City is not so far from my home town of Jonquière, I was missing my family a lot and I was jumping on any opportunity to go see them on weekends. Between Quebec and Jonquière there is the beautiful and popular Laurentian Park. Unfortunately, this area is also known to be a deadly one. Car accidents or a car hitting a moose are things that you see quite a lot in that area.

I hardly ever thought about that on my drive, since most of the time I was making the trip home with the most handsome man I had ever seen. I had a huge crush on him for many years. We were four students who always travelled together, everyone sitting always in the same spot in the car. I would always sit behind my handsome friend. That way I could look at his eyes in the rear-view mirror, smell his hair, and sometimes put my hand near his shoulder. I was absolutely crazy about him. Every time he would look in the rear-view mirror I would catch a glimpse of him and imagine some romantic scenario between the two of us.

On one occasion we were going back to Jonquière for a long weekend. We left on Friday and planned to come back on Sunday. None of us had class until the following Tuesday, but my lovely driver had to be back early because he had a group project to do on the Monday.

People in Saguenay-Lac-Saint-Jean have a reputation as people who like to have fun and drink a little beer, so as soon as we arrived in Jonquière, I called a few of my friends and we decided to go out to a bar. I was far from sober when I saw a girl who also studied at Laval University, but was not travelling with us that weekend. She asked me if she could take my place in the car to go back to Quebec City because she was also working on a group project on Monday. I refused at first, giving her a stupid reason like I had to get back early to clean my apartment. I couldn't tell her that I didn't want to miss an opportunity to spend time with my cute driver friend. She was disappointed, but all is fair in love and war so I didn't felt too guilty.

The Saturday night we went out again, drinking more than on the Friday, and once more I saw my friend from Laval. Again she asked to take my place in the car, and again I said no. This time she offered to pay half of my bus ticket to get back to Quebec City, telling me that I would have the chance to spend more time with my family if I were only leaving town on Monday. She gave me her phone number in case I should change my mind the next morning. I told her not to count on it and that I wasn't going to change my mind.

I can't really remember how I got back to my parent's house

that night, since I was really drunk. I know of course that I didn't drive! I fell asleep really quickly and I began to dream about my great grandmother who had died a few years before. I had never dreamt about her before and I've never dreamt about her since. In my dream, she was pleading with me to let the young lady take my place in the car. That way I could have fun spending more time with my parents and even go to lunch with my grandfather, her son. When I woke up the next morning, this dream was still fresh and clear in my memory, so during breakfast I asked my mother if she could help me pay the other half of my bus ticket if I would stay one more day. She said yes, and that it would be a pleasure to have me with them a little bit longer. I called the girl from Laval and I let her know she could have my place in the car back to school. She was overjoyed. After I hung up with her, I called the handsome driver and explained to him my decision and where he could pick up the girl who would be taking my place.

It was a beautiful sunny day and I had a wonderful time with my family… until we came back home that evening. A friend had called the house numerous times, and when I called her back wondering what the problem was, I was in for a terrible shock. She told me "Oh my god! I'm so happy you're ok!" I asked why she would say that, and she explained that the car I was supposed to be in had ended up in a terrible accident. I asked if everyone was okay. She said that it was a miracle that anyone survived the accident. Everyone in the car was safe except for one passenger who was killed in the accident. I was shocked and asked who it was. She said it was the girl who had taken my place and that, in the car, she had been sitting in my usual spot: right behind the driver. A large truck took a curve too fast and hit their car exactly where she was sitting.

Since that terrible day, on that very stretch of road, people sometimes see a girl who waves at them and signals to them to drive more slowly. I once had the chance to talk with a truck driver who saw this ghost. I asked him to describe to me the young lady he saw. It was the exact description of the girl who took my place on the way back to Laval. When I think about it, I am so sad for this girl and her family, but I can't stop thinking that there is a ghost in the Laurentians...and that ghost was supposed to be me.

The Ottawa Jail Hostel, formerly the Carleton County Jail

Ghosts at the Gallows: The Ottawa Jail Hostel

Hidden in plain sight between the bustling Rideau Centre Shopping Mall and the University of Ottawa campus is an impressive stone building older than Canada itself. Today this building is home to Hostelling International's Ottawa Jail Hostel, a place where visitors from around the world often stay while in Ottawa. At one time the building offered an entirely different kind of accommodation to its guests. Opened in 1862, the Carleton County Gaol (or jail) was in its day the pride of Ottawa, and was held up as a shining example of how all county jails across the province should be built.

For a number of years before the new jail opened, the four-room basement of the courthouse (which was located next door to the site of the jail) was used to hold prisoners. This set-up was less than ideal, as with no walls surrounding the building, passersby could easily converse with or pass items through the windows to the inmates. In fact, just before this dungeon was closed one inspector described it as "truly a very mockery of a prison....The dingy cells off the corridor are damp and unwholesome. The privy...was overflowing with abomination and sends out a stench that poisons alike the prison and Court House." Shortly after the

Carleton County Jail opened, the board of inspectors commented that the new jail was "probably the best in Canada, and the old jail was probably about the very worst."

The opening of the jail in 1862 marked a significant change in the role of law enforcement in Ottawa. Before the jail opened, particularly in the early days of Bytown, the city had a reputation for being a rough-and-tumble frontier town. In fact, early Bytown was known as one of the most dangerous towns in North America. With no real police presence, and without any legitimate jail or facilities to hold prisoners, justice and retribution were often handed out by the citizens themselves.

With the city more-or-less equally divided among the English, Irish, French, and Scottish communities, there was often significant religious and ethnic tension and conflict. Gangs became very prevalent, with the most feared being the "Shiners". The Shiners were a notorious gang that recruited Irish immigrants who had come to Ottawa to work on the Rideau Canal. When the Canal was completed in 1832, many of these labourers found themselves out of work, and took to passing the time at the local pubs or taverns, enjoying glass after glass of potato whiskey. In 1835 the Shiners began a bloody and violent campaign to drive the French Canadians out of Bytown, in the hopes that there would be more paying work left over for everyone else. The Shiners would threaten their families, assault them in the streets and do everything to make their lives miserable.

The Shiners grew so powerful that they began to intimidate the British residents of Upper Town as well, threatening or robbing them as they pleased. On one occasion, a pregnant British woman and her daughters were attacked in their sleigh by a group of Shiners. In her attempt to escape the attack, the woman became tangled in the outside frame of the sleigh, and was dragged along the frozen ground, with Shiners running alongside and beating her with sticks. They took the sleigh and horses, but eventually released the terrified family. The next morning the horses were found wandering the streets, their ears and tails cut off. The brutality of the Shiners is just one example of the lawlessness that was common in Ottawa right up until the 1860's.

One of the reasons Ottawa was such a rough place to live in the early days was the fact that there was no official police force in the town for its first forty years. Because there was no courthouse or jail, accused criminals would have to be taken through the woods on the long trek to Perth. Perth is only about an hour away by car today, but in those days it would have been a full day's journey by carriage. Along the way, suspected criminals would often be freed by a gang of friends and supporters and could easily escape into Lower Canada, or Quebec as it is now known. There were a handful of volunteer constables who could arrest people for unruly behaviour, but they did not hold much authority. Often, they would be given a physical demonstration of just how little power they had! One volunteer was assaulted and shot at, and an attempt was made to burn down his house. Another constable was waylaid at night and badly beaten by a group of men, suffering a broken collarbone. It was a pretty thankless job.

At one period in 1835, out of sixteen constables in Bytown only four were remained willing actually to arrest people. If they did arrest someone, they would have to transport the accused person to Perth at their own trouble and expense. The result of this system was that most disputes were handled locally by one of the many gangs operating here in Ottawa, and the official authorities were hardly ever involved.

When the new jail was finally built to serve this desperate need for law and order, it was intentionally designed to be an imposing and intimidating structure that would convey a sense of authority. The building is a prime example of English Georgian architecture, with its emphasis on symmetry and proportion that evoke notions of austerity and strength. The use of heavy stone along the foundation of the building creates an increased sense of mass and power. The chimneys, stonework, dormer windows and buttresses were all designed to reinforce this impression of authority.

Throughout its history, the jail was used for those serving both short-term and long-term sentences, as well as for those awaiting court appearances. Any sentence of less than two years would be served at the county jail. If the sentence were longer, the prisoner would usually be transferred to the federal penitentiary in Kingston, Ontario. Prisoners who had been sentenced to death would also be held at the jail until their execution. So in this building, at any given time, you might have people thrown in for the night on "drunk and disorderly" charges living right alongside prisoners who had been convicted of or were awaiting trial on much more serious charges.

Women were also imprisoned in the building, and, if they had children who could not be cared for, the children would also be housed in the jail. Female prisoners were treated slightly less severely than the male prisoners, and lived in dormitory-style accommodations. They had access to a bathtub and a washroom, and were watched over by a female guard known as the matron.

Children convicted of crimes, some as young as seven years old, were housed in the jail alongside the regular inmates. Having all these different inmates mixing together came to be seen as a major shortcoming of the building, particularly in regard to the children. One inspector in the 1880s was convinced that young people "started out on the most criminal and desolate course of life after associations formed from temporary incarceration for trifling offences here in the jail, and ultimately have graduated as matured criminals."

The mentally ill were also often kept at the jail while awaiting transfer to the asylum in Kingston, as there simply was no other safe place to keep them. The guards and officials at the jail were not sufficiently trained to deal with the unique challenges these inmates provided. On more than one occasion there were investigations launched after a mentally ill individual died while in custody at the jail.

By 1946, jail inspectors were criticizing the building as a "monstrous relic of an imperfect civilization where cells are medieval, incredibly cramped, with conditions far below the limits of human decency." The sixty tiny single-person cells, which were nicknamed "the drums" because of their small size and shape, were only three feet wide and nine feet deep, lacked electric light, and had only metal pails, known as "honey buckets" for toilet facilities. Manual labour was performed in the jail until the mid-1900s; after that, with no other rehabilitation or recreational facilities, there was little to occupy the inmates' time. This boredom was oppressive and occasionally caused prisoners to act out or riot in an attempt to break the monotony.

The jail was finally closed in 1972, after 110 years of service, due to its inhumane living conditions. Throughout its tenure the jail's reputation had gradually shifted from that of an exemplar of modern-day jail construction to an antiquated, archaic, and barbaric relic of the past. Within the city of Ottawa there was much debate as to what to do with the building once the jail had closed. The suggestions ranged from transforming it into a museum, to demolishing the entire building and putting up a parking lot in its place. We are thankful that this unique gem of Ottawa and Canadian history was saved when an agreement was reached with Heritage Canada and the Canadian Youth Hostels Association to transform the old jail into a hostel. The conversion of the building consisted of improving the ventilation, adding additional showers and washroom facilities, updating the kitchen, and creating larger family and private rooms. The total cost of renovating the building was around $200,000, some $140,000 more than it originally cost to build in 1862.

In August of 1973 the hostel opened its doors for business. Since that time it has developed a reputation as being one of the most haunted buildings in North America, and has been featured on many television programs, and in a variety of books, as an internationally renowned haunted spot. Many guests continue to go out of their way to stay at the hostel in the hope of having a unique supernatural experience of their own.

A number of years ago a group of four young men from Germany was travelling together and decided to spend the night at the hostel. The next morning they went down to the front desk and demanded their money back, because they had not seen a ghost. The desk clerk tried to explain that they paid their money to spend the night – not to see ghosts. He also tried to explain that he could not summon ghosts at will. The men became angry and insisted that their money be refunded. They became more hostile and abusive when the clerk denied their request. In the middle of all this shouting, a coin rose out of the open cash register and levitated at eye level in front of the five surprised witnesses. The coin stayed in the same place for a solid five seconds and then dropped to the floor. The young men, stunned into silence, picked up their luggage and left without another word (or their refund), their ghostly request having been answered in quite an unexpected way.

Who or what is responsible for the unusual activity in the Ottawa Jail Hostel is a matter of some debate. What is certain is that many people died while in custody at the jail from disease, suicide, exposure, abuse, or simply execution. Many of these individuals would have spent their final moments in extreme anguish and misery.

Some guests of the hostel have awoken in the middle of the night to see a ghostly figure standing or even sitting on the edge of their bed, reading what appears to be a Bible. While it would be shocking to make such a discovery, what makes it even more intriguing is that all descriptions of the apparition have been very similar. From those descriptions, the ghostly figure seems closely to resemble Patrick James Whelan, the first man to be taken to the gallows at the jail.

Whelan's tragic story began in the early hours of the morning on April 7th, 1868, when the Honourable Thomas D'Arcy McGee was shot and killed as he was about to enter his boarding house. Mr. McGee was a well-known politician, a close friend of Sir John A. MacDonald, and one of the Fathers of Confederation. He was well-loved in Parliament and was an excellent public speaker.

On the night of McGee's murder, the House of Commons had debated until 2:00AM. When McGee returned to his boarding house on Sparks Street he found that the door was bolted from the inside. Mrs. Trotter, his landlady, was waiting for her 13 year-old son, a parliamentary page, to return home, when she heard someone trying to open the door. She undid the bolt and just as she opened the door a crack, there was a blast from outside. She slammed the door shut and ran upstairs to get help. When she returned with several boarders, they opened the door and found McGee's murdered body on the steps. He had been shot at close range in the back of the head. McGee's false teeth were later discovered at the end of the front hall, as they had been shot right out of his mouth. Mrs. Trotter had opened the door at the exact moment the shot was fired, and her dressing gown was splattered with McGee's blood. The bullet was lodged in the doorway and later recovered by the police as evidence. Mrs. Trotter didn't see the killer when she opened the door, and when her son came home only a moment later, there was no-one on the street. Of the many people who began to crowd around McGee's body, none had seen any sign of the murderer.

Many of McGee's outraged friends and colleagues recalled the seemingly foreboding nature of his final public speech: "I hope that in this house mere temporary or local popularity will never be the test by which to measure the worth or efficiency of a public servant. It is, Sir, my humble opinion, that the leader who is ready to meet the tide of temporary unpopularity, who is prepared, if need be, to sacrifice himself, who is ready not only to triumph with his principles but even to suffer for his principles, he is one who has proved himself, above all others."

Right away, the police suspected a group of Irish known as the Fenians. The Fenians were mostly Irish Americans who were fighting to free Ireland from British rule; at the time of the murder they had made it clear that one of their plans was to invade Canada and hold it hostage with the intention to exchange it for Ireland's freedom. They had launched several attacks from the U.S. border in previous years, and even though McGee was an Irishman, who had once been a rebel leader himself, he had spoken out publicly against them. Many of the Fenians thought McGee was a traitor, and there were quite a number of threats against his life, so it seemed likely they had something to do with his murder. The police arrested a dozen Irishmen right away, eventually releasing all but one – a man named Patrick James Whelan. Whelan was Irish, thought to be a Fenian, and was in the gallery of the House of Commons on that fateful night. That was enough to start building a case against him. There was a lot of circumstantial evidence against Whelan in the beginning, but as his trial wore on, this evidence started to crumble. For example, an eyewitness named Lacroix stepped forward after a large reward was offered, but six of his coworkers testified that he was a compulsive liar and only interested in the reward money.

Despite the lack of evidence, public opinion was very strong in this case, and the people wanted someone to be punished for this horrible crime. Sir John A. Macdonald, McGee's old friend and Canada's first Prime Minister, was a close friend of the prosecuting lawyer and even began coming to the trial each day and sitting beside the judge. One can imagine the impact this would have had on the jury, perhaps causing them to believe that they were expected to find Whelan guilty. At the end of the trial, despite the fact there was no reliable witness who could place Whelan at the scene of the crime, and that the evidence against him was largely circumstantial, Whelan was convicted and sentenced to hang for the assassination of Thomas D'Arcy McGee.

Whelan maintained his innocence right up until the very end. When the sentence was handed down, he turned to the judge and said "And yet all that, my lord, does not make me guilty". On February 11th, 1869 at the 11th hour, over 5,000 people turned out in a terrible snowstorm to watch Whelan hang. In Whelan's final address to the gathered crowd, he forgave any sins committed against him and he asked for forgiveness for any sins he had committed against anyone. His last words were: "God Save Ireland and God save my soul." And with that, Whelan dropped to his death.

Whelan's final request was that he be buried in his family's plot in Montreal. The judge initially agreed to this request, but after the execution was carried out, officials became worried that if Whelan's remains were brought back to Montreal the Irish there would riot in protest at what they saw as a rigged trial. The decision was made to bury Whelan in secrecy in the grounds of the jail. As Whelan was a devout Roman Catholic, officials attempted to have a priest come to the jail to perform the burial rites. After some discussion, the priest refused to provide the sacred service on the grounds of a common jail. Whelan was placed in an unmarked grave and buried without ceremony. Years later, when the Mackenzie King Bridge was being built alongside the jail, several unmarked graves were discovered, and it is possible there are several more, perhaps even Patrick Whelan's included, under what is the Jail Hostel's parking lot today. If so, it would uniquely fulfill Whelan's final prophecy that no grass would grow upon his grave.

Many people are convinced that the restless spirit in the Ottawa Jail Hostel is that of Patrick James Whelan. Consider that Whelan may well have been an innocent man, executed for a crime he did not commit. In addition to that, he was buried on the grounds of the jail, against his wishes and without proper ceremony, despite promises made to him before his death. Many believe that Whelan continues to haunt the jail to make known the injustices that were committed against him.

In 2002 a distant relative of Patrick Whelan conducted a

Patrick James Whelan, hanged for the murder of D'Arcy McGee

The eighth floor cell block at the Ottawa Jail Hostel

ceremony at the jail, in an attempt to put his spirit to rest. They took some earth from the courtyard and buried it in Montreal in his family plot. Ever since that ceremony, encounters at the jail have become even more frequent. Either the other spirits here were feeling ignored, or Whelan is intent on sending a message that he has not left the building.

While most people believe the strange activities that take place within the building are attributable to Whelan, not everyone believes that he is the ghost in question. Although the majority of the supernatural activity in the jail has posed no immediate physical threat to the participants, on occasion there are events that suggest a more diabolical and frightening presence. In the 1980's a hostel employee was up on death row when a heavy steel door suddenly slammed shut with great force, cutting off one of her fingers. As the door was large, heavy and not easily closed, there was no simple explanation as to what had happened. More recently, as the staff of the hostel was sitting down for a meeting, one of the managers felt she had been slapped in the face by an invisible hand. The blow was of sufficient force to cause a red mark upon her face and her eyes to water. The other members of the staff who witnessed the event were at a loss to explain what had transpired.

One woman who came on our Haunted Walk a few years ago recounted her terrifying experience to us. She and her husband were led on a private tour through the jail. She told us that she found the building itself creepy overall, but that the feeling intensified when they reached the gates on the eighth floor. She felt a strong urge to flee, and told the tour guide that she did not feel comfortable going any further. He told her that the tour was almost over and that it would only be a short distance to get out, shorter than backtracking through the building. They continued, and while waiting in the area outside death row, the woman felt as if the air was being pulled from her lungs. She was extremely uncomfortable and told the group she wanted to leave right away. The tour guide led them to the doorway leading into the gallows. The woman had great difficulty entering the stairwell and at the top of the stairs, her discomfort grew to a feeling of terror, as she felt several sets of hands thumping on her back as if to push her down the stairs. For what felt like several minutes, she could not move because of this terrible feeling. She described the feeling as if she were being "hit on the back by several people at the same time". Finally she was able to continue downstairs and exit into the courtyard. She told her guide that she felt as if they had not been alone in the stairwell, and that whatever it was wanted them "out of there".

In 2003, a school group was being led on a tour through the hostel. Two boys were horsing around while the tour was finishing up. Some of the children became convinced that Whelan might be buried right beneath a slab of concrete under the gallows, and two of the boys began to jump up and down on it. They were laughing and joking as they jumped on what they thought was Whelan's burial place. After a moment, they suddenly stopped. The boys turned to face the group, and everyone could clearly see that they had both been struck with nosebleeds at exactly the same time. There was no apparent explanation, and while it may have been seen as a rather remote coincidence at the time, this was not the last time this has happened. Since that incident, on a number of separate occasions, our guides have found while telling this story that a customer on the tour has suddenly developed a nosebleed. On each occasion they seemed genuinely surprised and perhaps not entirely happy to have the opportunity to share in one of the ghost stories. These encounters could indicate the presence of the restless spirit of Patrick Whelan, but there is another, perhaps more disturbing possibility.

Some believe that the more frightening encounters at the jail may be the handiwork of the ghost of Eugene Larment, the third and final prisoner executed at the jail. Larment's life was a difficult struggle and he often found himself in trouble with the law. Growing up, Larment's parents had a very rocky relationship, with his father eventually leaving his mother due to her "misconduct." In a dysfunctional home, Larment did not have the support and boundaries necessary for healthy development. He rarely attended school, and often stole and committed other petty crimes which were rumoured to have been tolerated, if not encouraged, by his mother.

His criminal career (which included charges of vagrancy, breaking and entering, as well as armed robbery) came to an end in the early morning hours of October 24th, 1945. That evening Larment and two of his accomplices had been attempting to steal cars from the area around Parliament Hill. A night watchman, having observed the three men at work, called the police. Detective Thomas Stoneman and Constable Russell Berndt of the Ottawa City Police Department arrived on the scene and immediately approached the three men. Eugene Larment drew a nickel-plated revolver (one of a handful of weapons the trio had stolen from the Canadian War Museum the night before), and from a distance of six to eight feet, shot Detective Stoneman. After firing at the detective, Larment spun and fired unsuccessfully in the direction of Constable Berndt, who had taken cover in the entrance of a hotel. A wild foot chase ensued, with all three men eventually being arrested. As a result of his injuries, Detective Stoneman passed away in hospital five days later.

The three suspects were held in the jail and with just over a week before their trial was to begin, they made a daring escape attempt. With the aid of a broom handle, they managed to overpower three guards, stealing their keys and locking them into cells. As they moved to the main stairs, they were confronted by several guards. While one of the prisoners distracted the guards, the other two uncoiled a fire hose and used the powerful jet of water to force the guards to retreat down the stairs. With police reinforcements on the way, this was as far as Larment and his accomplices got, still two flights up in the jail, with three heavy barred doors between them and freedom.

During his trial, Larment tried several defenses; first he claimed that he was too drunk to be held accountable for his actions; then that he had shot in self-defense; and, finally, he tried to blame his criminal behaviour on his poor and troubled upbringing. Nevertheless, he was convicted and was hanged on March 26, 1946, at the Carleton County Jail. Larment's accomplices, Wilfrid d'Amour and Albert Henderson, received 27 and 29 years respectively in the Kingston Penitentiary.

While the ghosts of Patrick Whelan and Eugene Larment do seem to be plausible candidates for some of the hauntings at the jail, some experiences are so strange and extreme that it is difficult to even hazard a guess as to who or what may be behind them. In 2005, a hostel guest approached one of our tour guides, who was giving a historical tour of the jail. She wanted to know if there where any ghost stories about the building, as the previous night she had had a very disturbing encounter. She went on to explain that late in the evening she had returned to her room on the fourth floor to get ready for bed. As she ducked into her room to grab her toothbrush, out of the corner of her eye she saw what she thought was another hosteller standing in the washroom down the hall wrapped in a large white towel. As she walked toward the washroom, the figure remained in place, until she was just outside the washroom door. All at once she had a horrible dark feeling in the pit of her stomach. It was just then that the figure slowly began to turn toward her. To her horror she realized this mysterious figure did not have a face, but rather a blank smooth slate without any expression. There were no facial features at all where a nose, a mouth and eyes should be. The hosteller quickly made her way back to the TV lounge where she knew there were other people awake. When she made it downstairs, she began to ask if everyone was alright, or if there had been some kind of accident, as this dark feeling inside of her was still so strong. When she explained what had happed, several hostellers took her keys and ran up to the fourth floor to investigate. Nothing, and no one, was ever found. The next day she moved into a private room with her friend, refusing to spend another night alone on the fourth floor.

There is a controversial theory to explain these unusually intense and extreme experiences. Over the years there has been speculation that unofficial executions took place at the jail, particularly in the early days, at the hands of the guards. Supporters of this notion often point to a wooden beam, which runs directly above the back stairs and seems to have no architectural purpose, which could have served as a makeshift gallows. On this beam there are some suspicious marks that arguably could be rope burns. It is difficult to say what exactly caused these indentations. These marks may well be the result of secret executions, or just as easily could be marks caused by ropes hauling heavy objects (furniture, cell doors) up the stairs, with the beam being used like a primitive pulley system. As there would have been no records kept of unofficial executions, it is a rumour that is very difficult to confirm or deny. However, if inmates were illegally and secretly executed at the jail, it may go a long way to explaining some of the paranormal activity experienced in the building. Perhaps the faceless ghost was just that, the spirit of an inmate whose death was long forgotten or was shrouded in secrecy.

The Ottawa Jail Hostel has a tremendous reputation, not only as a one-of-a-kind place to stay, but as one of the most haunted buildings in North America. Guests from around the world come to stay at the hostel, many hoping for their own unique encounter with the restless spirits in the building. There is no way of predicting when the next brush with the supernatural will occur. Certainly it is a building that is well worth a visit and an experience not to be missed.

Friday's Roast Beef House Restaurant

Culinary Spirits:
Ottawa's Haunted Restaurants

Ottawa is home to many excellent and well-known restaurants. With so many political visitors and leisure travellers, the dining establishments are as diverse as the clientele that visits them. In downtown Ottawa, there are two particular areas where diners often congregate: the Byward Market and Elgin Street.

Both of these areas have unique and rich histories. The Byward Market has been an active commercial hub of activity since the early days of Bytown. Riots, fires, murders, and brothels have all played a role in the history of the Market. Today, the Market is one of the most popular entertainment districts in Ottawa. Boasting a large number of restaurants and exciting nightlife, the Market has something for everyone, from the jazz connoisseur to the university student to the lover of fine food and drink.

One of the most interesting historic locations in the Market is Clarendon Court, a courtyard that is now surrounded by several excellent restaurants, but originally was home to hotels, shops, pubs and "houses of ill-repute". The building, home to the Courtyard Restaurant since 1980, was originally the site of the McArthur Hotel. There is a well-known rumour that Clarendon

Court was the site of a military hanging during the Fenian Crisis, but there seems to be very little factual evidence to back this up. That being said, the strange events that continue to take place in the Courtyard Restaurant suggest something very unusual may be going on in those buildings.

Most of the encounters in the restaurant have taken place on the second floor which houses a loft room and a private dining room. Many of the staff members have described a very uncomfortable feeling whenever they find themselves alone on the second floor. They describe it as an overwhelming sense of being unwelcome, as though someone is up there who very much wants them to leave. Staff members have refused to close up the restaurant at night, or have decided to just leave items behind that they have forgotten upstairs, rather than spend any time alone up there. Occasionally lights will turn on or off, or all of the equipment at the bar will start up at the same time. However, the staff are most convinced simply by the strong feelings of discomfort they get from being on that floor.

The manager of the restaurant was closing up one night when she walked into the loft room and saw a woman standing in the far corner of the room. The woman was dressed in Victorian clothing and was just standing there quietly gazing out the window. The manager stepped back in fright and looked again to find that the strange woman had completely disappeared. A number of years later another staff member who was closing a different section of the second floor spotted this same woman. Again she was standing and looking out the window, and did not even look up or notice him at all. Neither got a very good look at her face, but both described her clothing as old-fashioned and in a Victorian style.

One staff member was always very skeptical about the

stories surrounding the restaurant. She believed that they were just being told to scare the new staff, and assumed that they came from nothing more than over-active imaginations, or perhaps the odd practical joke. As a result, she would happily take the late night shifts and never had anything unusual happen to her on the second floor. One night she was closing that part of the restaurant when she heard some footsteps coming towards her down the hallway. There was absolutely no one there, but she very clearly felt someone brush up against her as the footsteps walked straight past her. She very calmly walked downstairs to the kitchen, opened a drawer, took out the biggest knife she could find, sat down on the floor and called her boyfriend to come and get her.

After a bit of research we found one possible explanation for the haunting at the Courtyard Restaurant: in 1872, a terrible fire raged through the area, destroying a good portion of the block. Several people were caught in the fire, but almost all managed to get out alive. Only one woman, Mrs. Evans, was unable to escape. She had gone back to her bedroom for some personal papers and was killed in the fire. Onlookers could hear her screaming but were unable to find her in the thick smoke and flames. Perhaps it is Mrs. Evans' spirit that is still trapped here, forever waiting for her rescue.

Another popular destination in downtown Ottawa is Elgin Street. In the early days of the city, the street was an area where many of the wealthier citizens would have had their homes. Today, Elgin Street is packed with many popular eateries, pubs, and clubs. However, if one looks carefully, traces of early Ottawa still remain. At 150 Elgin Street is Friday's Roast Beef House, a beautifully preserved building from the early days of Confederation. The building is also known as Grant House, since it was originally built for Doctor James Grant in 1875. This would have been one of the better houses on the block- it cost a very hefty $11,000 to build, at a time when an average house cost under $5,000. In addition to being his home, Grant also ran his practice out of the building, even using the basement as his morgue.

James Grant was born in Inverness, Scotland on August 11th, 1831. Only a few weeks after his birth, the family moved to Glengarry, Ontario (about 1 hour south-east of Ottawa) where his father quickly established himself as one of the area's most distinguished doctors. Young James went on to Queen's University in Kingston for his undergraduate studies, eventually graduating from McGill in Montreal as a medical doctor in 1854. Soon after graduation, Dr. Grant established a practice in Ottawa. On January 22nd, 1856, Dr. Grant married Maria Malloch and together they had twelve children. Due to his renowned medical skill and tireless work ethic, his practice became very successful and attracted many of the most prominent members of the Ottawa community. For his vast knowledge and interest in several scientific fields, he was made a charter member of the Royal Society of Canada. Dr. Grant was held in such high esteem that he served as the official physician to the Governor General of Canada from 1867 to 1905. In addition to his professional aspirations, he was also very involved in politics and twice served as a Member of Parliament for the Conservative Party (1867-74, 1893-96), taking part in the important debates that shaped the nation following Confederation. He was knighted "Sir" James Grant in 1880, in part for saving the life of Queen Victoria's daughter, Princess Louise, after her sleigh overturned near Rideau Hall. James Alexander Grant passed away on June 5th, 1920 at the age of 88, having lived at his home on Elgin Street for 45 years. Perhaps it should not come as a surprise that when strange things started to happen in the building, everyone assumed it was the ghost of Doctor Grant.

Most of the encounters in the building have taken place in the second and third-floor hallways. Members of the restaurant staff have heard footsteps descending the stairs long after the building has closed. Others have had trays knocked out of their hands, and more than one patron has fallen sideways over the banister on the staircase, claiming to have been pushed by unseen hands. A woman who came on our tour told us that this had happened to her before we had a chance to tell this part of the story, and was very shocked when we told her it had happened several times before.

An elderly man has been seen sitting at a second floor window on numerous occasions after the building was closed. Late at night, many of the staff will hear the sound of laughter coming from the piano bar upstairs after everyone else has left, or hear the sound of their name being called from an empty room. Perhaps most convincing are the reports that both staff and guests have heard the sound of someone breathing right next to them. They describe it as a deep wheezing with an occasional cough. What many of them do not know is that Grant suffered from severe asthma all his life, and so it seems that he would make a likely candidate to be the spirit who has been haunting the place all these years.

Laurier House National Historic Site

Laurier House

Since 1951, starting with Louis St. Laurent, all elected Canadian prime ministers have resided at 24 Sussex Drive. Before that time there was no official residence, and previous prime ministers lived at a variety of different locations around Ottawa. Most notable of these is Laurier House, which served as home to both Sir Wilfrid Laurier and William Lyon Mackenzie King. Many foreign dignitaries have attended receptions and other formal functions at Laurier House, including King George VI, Charles de Gaulle, Franklin D. Roosevelt, and Sir Winston Churchill. Given the building's unique history, and the powerful, charismatic characters who have walked its halls, many people believe the building to be haunted by restless spirits from the past.

In 1850, John Leslie, a jeweller, bought property on the eastern outskirts of Ottawa. After Confederation, the area became known as "Sandy Hill", a new and trendy neighbourhood for businessmen and politicians. John Leslie waited until 1878 before building a house on the property. The house was built in the Second Empire style to match the other fine homes in this fast-growing community. His family lived in the house until 1896.

In 1874, Wilfrid Laurier became a Member of Parliament. At that time, he was still living in Arthabaska, Quebec and would come to Ottawa only when the House of Commons was in session.

Laurier was the first French-Canadian to serve as prime minister. When he became prime minister in 1896, he moved to the capital full-time. Since he was not wealthy enough to buy a house suitable for a man of his position, the Liberal party organized a fundraiser and, in 1897, bought the house located at 335 Theodore Street for their leader. Laurier was in power from 1896 to 1911, a time of growth, industrialization, and substantial immigration in Canada. Throughout his career he always tried to find a compromise between the interests of both English-Canadian imperialists and French-Canadian nationalists. Also under his leadership, in 1905, Alberta and Saskatchewan joined Confederation, and Canada was able to achieve greater autonomy from Great Britain.

Over the years, Theodore Street changed its name to Laurier Avenue in honour of its famous resident. Laurier added a few elements to the house, like the verandah, and an extension to the second floor for the servants. Laurier and his wife, Zoé, enjoyed their life at the house. They would often invite their friends and family over, organizing receptions or relaxing with their pets. The Prime Minister was often seen reading in his studio, while Zoé preferred playing piano in her morning room in the company of her pet birds.

Laurier lived in the house until his death in 1919. After Zoé's death two years later, she bequeathed the house to her husband's successor as leader of the Liberal party, William Lyon Mackenzie King, who made several important renovations before taking up residence in 1923. The roofs were redone, the walls re-painted, the floors changed, and an elevator was added. But the most important renovation was the transformation of the billiard room on the third floor into King's personal library.

Mackenzie King loved Laurier House and considered it a

refuge from political life. Unlike the Lauriers, King would rarely organize receptions at the house. He was a solitary man, preferring to work in his library, surrounded by his books. When he did organize receptions, they were always for political purposes, such as to entertain diplomats and state leaders. Unlike Wilfrid Laurier, King preferred working from home even when the House of Commons was in session. He would lock himself in the library to work on state affairs and would only go to Parliament in the afternoon.

King was Canada's longest-serving Prime Minister, and held office for a total of 22 years in the first half of the 20th century. The extraordinary details of Mackenzie King's private life were only revealed after his death, with the release of his personal diaries to the public.

Throughout his life, King had a passion for literature. In 1893, when he was a student at the University of Toronto, he began to keep a daily diary. He published many books, but his diaries are considered one of the greatest literary treasures in Canada. Until his death in 1950, Mackenzie King described all aspects of his personal life, political events, and his reflections on countless subjects in his diaries. These one-of-a-kind documents not only describe the political history of Canada in the first half of the 20th century, but also illustrate the intriguing private life of a compelling Prime Minister.

King managed to hide almost all of his eccentricities during his lifetime, as it was his greatest fear that his interest in spiritualism (contacting and speaking with the spirits of the dead) would have been seen to have negatively influenced his political decisions or his ability to run the country. King, at first, treated spiritualism as a passing interest, attending séances and using mediums to make contact with the spirit of his departed mother, whom he missed dearly. He also interpreted his dreams, read his fortune in tea leaves, and studied numerology.

Over the years, his interest grew to the point where he was travelling out of town to attend séances, and even took a break from talks with Winston Churchill to visit a medium in London. He claimed to have made contact with many members of his family, but also with several famous figures including Laurier, Theodore Roosevelt, Lincoln, Anne Boleyn and even Queen Victoria, all of whom had kind words to say about the way he was running the country.

Another recurring theme in Mackenzie King's diary was his love for his dog, Pat. Never married, and childless, Mackenzie King devoted his attention to his dogs. Although he had three dogs with the name Pat, the first one, who lived from 1924 to 1941, was certainly the most beloved.

King had always been superstitious, and superstition played an important part in his life. On the one hand, he stuck to certain unusual beliefs, such as his belief in omens, because of which he would only sign bills when the hands on the clock were exactly aligned: this meant that a deceased loved one was watching over him. He would constantly look for signs of the future in birth dates and numbers. The most important numbers for him were 7 and 17. When the Second World War ended in Europe on May 7th, 1945, King saw this date as an interesting sign. His birthday was on December 17th and his dog died at the age of 17. He then wrote in his diary: "He has been at my side all that time, that number is his and mine." (July 12th, 1941)

On the other hand, he was also a very religious man. He believed in heaven and in life after death. When four members of his family died a few years apart (his sister Bella in 1915, his father

Sir Wilfrid Laurier, taken around 1900

Mackenzie King with painting of his mother, at Laurier House.

in 1916, his mother in 1917 and his brother in 1922), he found comfort in the fact that he would see them again in the afterlife. He also gave religious counsel to his dog Pat, teaching him how to be a good Christian and reading to him from the Bible. One cannot help but wonder if Pat was very interested.

Despite all of this odd behaviour, it does seem to be true that Mackenzie King did not allow his private beliefs to colour his political decisions. On no occasion did King seek the advice of the spirits, his dogs or his mother on matters of national policy. He was an effective Prime Minister, and managed to avoid major scandals while in office, which is more than we can say for many of our other national leaders. It may be the final irony that Canada's longest-running Prime Minister was secretly also the most eccentric of all.

When he died in 1950, Mackenzie King bequeathed the house to all Canadians. Laurier House is now managed as a museum by Parks Canada and has been preserved as it was when Mackenzie King lived there.

It comes as little surprise that Laurier House is considered to be a haunted building; with all of the table-rapping and spirit summoning that took place in the building, not to mention its rich political history, it would perhaps be more astonishing if some of the ghosts did not stick around.

Mackenzie King kept a picture of his mother in every room of the house. In the library on the third floor he had a small shrine dedicated to her, at which he left a fresh flower every day. In front of her picture there was a small decorative box with her wedding ring and a lock of her hair. He was said to have spoken to her spirit every night before bed. This room is also home to his famous crystal ball, although there is no evidence that he ever actually used it for anything other than decoration.

One of the Parks Canada guides who used to work in Laurier House said that he believes the building is haunted. One night, at the end of his shift, he began turning out the lights in the building, starting from the top floor and working his way down to the bottom floor. He was surprised to hear a noise from the top floor and rushed up the stairs to find that a light beside the shrine to Mackenzie King's mother had been turned back on. It is said that this light was always the last one that Mackenzie King would turn out before bed, as he would say goodnight to his mother.

On another occasion, a photographer and her friend were doing a photo shoot in the building, after hours, in that very same room. The security guard, who was with the group, was anxiously waiting for his replacement, who was running late. He asked if the others would mind if he left early. They said they did not, and he left. Several minutes later, the two women clearly heard the back door open and close, and footsteps coming up the stairs. They assumed it was the second guard, but when they looked they found that no one was there. The guard arrived about ten minutes later, knowing nothing about the noises they had heard. The back door was locked and there was no way anyone could have crept past the women without them noticing. What made this interesting to the staff of the museum is that Mackenzie King was said to have used the back door when he was sneaking home from a late night séance. Some people believe that it may even be the ghost of Mackenzie King himself, keeping an eye on his home, to make sure it is being used in the way that he intended. We are happy to report that the house has been preserved as a National Historic Site, and welcomes visitors from across Canada and around the world. It is an important place to visit for anyone who has an interest in ghosts or Canadian history.

Gatineau River, Before 1882

The Gatineau Ghost Story
A Ghost Investigation by Margo (tour guide)

As a long-standing tour guide and head of our Ghost Investigation Unit, Margo is very familiar with many of the spookier places in the Ottawa area. This did not prevent her from getting a chill when hearing this melancholy tale of an old log home along the banks of the Gatineau River.

It's a hot July night in 2001. Jeff and I are out on our first assignment as part of the Haunted Walk's newly formed Ghost Investigation Unit. We are to conduct an interview with the owner of a haunted property whom Jeff had met quite by chance. And we are lost – somewhere in Quebec, we know that much, having crossed the bridge over from Ottawa into Gatineau some time ago, but otherwise we have no idea how near to or far from our destination we are, nor the first idea of how to get there. Some investigators we are turning out to be! We have no map and no contact information for the subject we are interviewing (these things have been forgotten in our zeal to remember the video camera and tape recorder). Our cell phones, it turns out, won't work out here in the middle of the wild Gatineau hills. Of course we only discovered these things after we were already some distance on our way. Jeff has been to the property in Cantley once before and is trying to get there now by memory. We've been driving around without success for a couple of hours and it's clear that we are going to need help to get us where we are going before the sun goes down.

Finally we see a house, a mint-green 1950s bungalow with a long, flat driveway. A woman, man and child are outdoors on the front lawn and seem to be doing some sort of yard work, though there is no shrubbery and there are very few flowers to be seen, just an expanse of green lawn. In any case, they are the first people we have seen in over half an hour – perhaps they can help. As Jeff turns into the driveway, all three look up and eye us suspiciously. Banjo music begins playing in both our imaginations. Jeff, a man who is not too scared to walk into a haunted building, is a little nervous about asking help from these strangers living in the middle of backwoods nowhere. He is braver than I am, though; he actually gets out of the car. I move into the driver's seat, ready to help make a fast getaway should one be needed, and roll down the window the better to hear the first signs of trouble. I watch Jeff make a friendly approach to the family who, thankfully, seem to be interested in helping. The little girl runs towards the car, something soft and fur-covered held in her arms. As she draws near, I see it is a white rabbit, with floppy brown ears. "This is my rabbit," she tells me with no introduction. "I used to have another one, but my dad killed it." "Oh, yes?" I say, making sure there's a smile on my face while, at the same time, slyly looking to see if the keys are still in the ignition. I begin anxiously looking for Jeff, who has gone into the house with the couple, so I'm not listening very well to the little girl who is telling me intensely, in accented English, about the horrors of the attack made on her now-deceased rabbit (was it a coyote? a dog? What did she just say?), but I do clearly hear her say, "So, my dad hit its head with a baseball bat." "Oh. Ah, that's too bad," I manage. I am thankful that Jeff returns to the car before the conversation can go much further. He waves goodbye to the couple as I move back into the passenger seat. "They were nice," he says. I just look at him. "A little creepy," he adds, "but nice." Turns out they knew the man we were trying to interview and were able to give Jeff the phone number and let him use the phone. "Jeff! Where the hell are you?" our subject laughed into the phone when he called. Turns out we were, in fact, completely lost and nowhere near where we should have been. Another half hour of driving, and we are finally (only two hours late!), carefully making our way down the steep gravel drive that leads to our interviewee's home in the woods on the shores of the Gatineau River.

A tall, elderly man, dressed in shorts and a casual shirt, greets us warmly when we finally knock at the door. Jeff introduces me. There are offers of coffee and brownies, and finally we are led down a narrow hallway and a few stairs into the sitting room. The house may be made entirely of logs, but this room might well belong to a cathedral. The ceiling is two storeys high, the back wall of the room made almost entirely of glass windows and sliding doors which lead out onto a deck looking over the river below. The view from the couch we sit on is all trees and water, the sun slowly setting over the hills in the distance. The gentleman settles into his armchair and smiles bemusedly at us as we struggle to get our borrowed equipment working. We quickly discover that he is hard of hearing and has difficulty hearing my voice, so Jeff sits on the end of the couch nearest him, holding the video camera, and will be the one to ask any questions. It soon becomes clear, however, that questions will not be necessary. This is a man well-used to being interviewed and telling stories. He has had a long career in politics, has been a researcher and a journalist, travelled the world, and hung out with famous people like Glenn Gould. I try to remember the ghost investigator's creed of careful examination and skepticism, but it's hard to be skeptical when your subject's Order of Canada is hanging on the wall behind him, next to photographs of himself standing with various world leaders. And when he so readily sympathizes with the ghost story researcher's plight, saying things like, "for every one story that is valid, there must be a dozen that are imagined." He assures us that any of the odd experiences he will relate will have had two witnesses or more. In the end, we decide just to let him speak and save any questions for later.

He begins. "This is the story of incidents which we don't understand, but which absorb us, which have happened on our property." He and his wife had moved to the property in the mid-1960's and began collecting old, abandoned log cabins (dating from 1819 to 1867) and moving them onto their land. These cabins were restored and lived in and were used to show people what life was like back in the early days of Canada. The property sits on the Gatineau River, close to Ottawa – Parliament Hill can be seen, on a clear day, from their highest point of land – "And yet," he says "we are still very close to the old frontier of Quebec." There had been no cabin on the land when they bought it, so they had had one built for themselves. One morning, just before dawn, he and his wife sat bolt upright in bed and looked at each other. "I'm sorry, I hope I didn't wake you. But I must have been dreaming," he said. "I heard footsteps. Very, very clearly. And they didn't make any sense. It must have been a dream because they were coming through that corner window – that's where they started – and they crossed the corner of the cottage floor and out the door." His wife replied, "Well, I heard exactly the same thing." And it turned out, this was not the first time she had heard the footsteps. The next day, they both went to the library and began researching ghosts and poltergeists. He learned that poltergeists often appear in houses occupied by girls entering puberty. At the time the couple had three daughters just about that age.

At this point we hear the front door being opened and stop recording for a few moments as the caretaker of the property, a quiet young man from Newfoundland, enters and is introduced. A moment later, I hear the door open again and footsteps down the hallway, but no one else enters the room. Someone must have come in and, not wanting to disturb us, ducked into one of the side rooms, I think. The caretaker joins us, sitting in an armchair. A big, black, shaggy dog gets up from where he had been lying and drops down at the caretaker's feet, quickly falling back asleep. The young man is well-acquainted with the strange goings-on of the property, having experienced a few himself. "How do you feel about that?" Jeff asks. "It's annoying," he says. He listens intently as we continue recording. The gentleman continues in his mild, baritone voice, dipping time and again away from the main story to tell us about the various interesting things he has learned in his research and travels. He sits with one long leg casually draped over the other, an unlit pipe in his hand.

The first of the antique log cabins to be purchased for the property dated from 1832, he tells us. The cabin was restored and offered to his wife's mother to live in. A day or two after her first night sleeping there she approached her daughter quite angrily one morning saying, "Why are you checking up on me?" Her daughter, however, had no idea what she could mean. "Well," her mother said, "I heard your footsteps last night downstairs in the log house. And they went right across from one of the windows to the door." Her daughter turned away so her mom wouldn't see her face and told her she must have been dreaming. She didn't want to frighten her mother by telling her what she really thought. The ghost had moved! The footsteps were never again heard in the bedroom of the main house, but the mother came on many different mornings to accuse her daughter, "There you were again last night! I don't know why you try sneaking up on me." But they never did tell her about the suspected ghost.

The gentleman tells us that he and his wife felt it important not to tell people about the ghost on the property. "We didn't want the story to get out because it would make it so hard to authenticate anything that happened in the future." (This man is a ghost investigator's dream!) And so they kept these stories to themselves.

As a Centennial project, they had the antique cabin furnished as it might have been in 1867. Afterwards, they began renting it out to a man who was, at that time, the head of the Political Science department at Carleton University. This man stayed alone on the property all winter while the others headed back to town. Occasionally the gentleman would ski in to check up on his tenant. His tenant began complaining about hearing footsteps almost right away. The gentleman decided not to tell him about other's experiences with these footsteps, and instead laughed it off, advising his tenant not to have so much rum and coffee. A few weeks later, however, his tenant said "Look, I really have to talk to you about this." He then went on to describe how a framed photograph of Queen Victoria, which was hanging on the wall had been behaving strangely. One night he woke up upon hearing a terrible commotion downstairs. He knew he was alone in the cabin, and the property itself was completely isolated in the winter. He came down the stairs expecting to see that some animal had somehow got inside the cabin, but instead saw that the photograph was swinging violently back and forth on its nail. It was the only picture moving. He sat down on the stairs and watched it swing more and more wildly until finally it jumped right off its nail and fell to the floor, the glass shattered. "And that was that," he said. "Everything was calm. I went back to bed." In the morning he cleaned up the glass and eventually replaced it, hanging the picture back up on the wall. But then one night it happened again. Once again he replaced the glass and hung it back up. And once again, the picture crashed to the floor in the night. This time, before he put it back up on the wall, he covered the photograph over with a tranquil painting of a snowy scene. The picture never moved again.

The gentleman and Jeff begin to speculate on why the ghost might have such an obvious dislike for Queen Victoria. Suddenly, I hear the sound of the front door opening again and footsteps down the hallway. Once again, I think nothing of it—that is, until I see that the caretaker has lifted his head abruptly and is listening. He gets up quietly and silently walks over to the stairs leading up into the hallway. The other two, still talking intently, have not noticed. The caretaker looks down the hallway and into the side room, but then turns around, heading back toward his chair. He sees me looking at him and shrugs his shoulders "Nothing there." "Yeah, that's what I was wondering," I say. But he just shrugs his shoulders again as if to say, "It happens all the time."

It is just the four of us, then, and a softly snoring dog, huddled together in one room of this large house. The sun is dipping ever more closely to the horizon, and I am already feeling fairly spooked, when I realize that what we have heard so far has only been a prelude. The crux of the tale is yet to come.

Many months later, the tenant of the old cabin had a friend staying with him. They woke up one night to find that the room was suddenly brilliantly lit up with a light that was bright enough to read by, but seemed to have no source. It lasted for less than a minute and disappeared. This happened on several different occasions. Then, one night, the tenant was away travelling and his friend was on her own in the cabin. She again woke up to a bright illumination in the room, but this time looked up to see the figure of a woman standing at the foot of the bed. The woman, she said, had straight black hair hanging down, dripping wet, and a very sad face. The woman just stood there, staring at her, giving off a feeling of tremendous sadness. After a few moments, the tenant's friend tried to speak to the woman, but she just disappeared. "Later on, that same figure – which I think we're entitled now to call a ghost – appeared when both our tenant and his friend were there, several times. Always the same way; just would stand there sadly."

The gentleman and his wife decided they might try asking the locals for old stories from the area, hoping in this way to discover some old tale that might explain who this woman might have been and why her ghost was haunting their property. They were careful not to let word of the ghost leak out, not wanting to influence the stories they might be told. It did not come right away, but eventually they began to hear of a story that seemed to click. The story tells how, in the early days of settlement in the area, a young native woman and a young man of European descent had fallen in love and wanted to be married. Unfortunately, due to the prejudices of the times, both their families were dead set against it. The couple then decided to elope by fleeing across the Gatineau River in a boat. "You'd never know it today, now that the river is flooded and quiet, but back before the dam was built, this area of the river was the shortest place to cross, but had some very dangerous rapids and was a treacherous, narrow, deep, raging stream." The couple tried to cross the river, but unfortunately, so the story goes, the woman fell out of the boat and was drowned in the attempt. The locals had heard tell of how, from time to time ever since, this unlucky woman's spirit was seen wandering the shores of the river.

After the initial sightings, her ghost was seen now and again by other tenants of the cabin and in other places on the property, but again, the gentleman insists, only these people and his family members knew about the goings-on. In this way, he felt, they could be sure any experiences those new to the property had were real, and not just imagined out of expectation.

"I'm going to jump ahead now, several years ahead." He tells us of how his 15-year old granddaughter one time brought to the property a friend who had never been there before. The two girls wandered around, touring the property, and eventually sat on a hill overlooking the cabin in which the woman's ghost had most frequently been seen. Suddenly, the granddaughter noticed that her friend had become completely lost in thought, just staring off at nothing. Knowing her friend to be a quiet, withdrawn young woman, the granddaughter did not think too much of it, but just waited. A few moments passed before her friend shook herself and said, "I'm very sorry, I just lost you. I'm terribly sorry, it's alright; I'm fine now." The granddaughter asked if she was sure she was alright, and her friend said yes, but then said, "Well, actually, I should tell you, I just saw a ghost." She went on to describe how a woman with long, black, dripping wet hair came and stood just in front of her. Though surprised, the granddaughter, of course, knew of the ghost on the property and was just about to tell her friend this, when her friend said, "Yes, she came and stood there. And then she spoke." The ghost had never spoken to anyone before, but the granddaughter's friend said the woman asked if she could speak to her and then said, "I'm so lonely and unhappy." The ghost then went on to tell the girl of how she and her fiancé had tried to escape across the river, to elope when their families would not let them marry. The waters were very rough, she said, and they were having a tremendous time keeping control of the boat. She began to despair and thought they would never make it across the river, when suddenly, they made it past the rapids to the calmer water on the other side and she realized they would make it after all. In her joy, she turned towards her fiancé just in time to see him reach out and push her into the water, where he held her under until she drowned.

When the woman had finished her story, she smiled at the girl and said, "I'm so glad to have told my story. Thank you." And then she disappeared. "And, to the best of my knowledge," the gentleman adds, "the ghost hasn't been seen since."

I think Jeff and I may have turned a bit pale as we shuddered. Even the dog seems to feel it – he rolls over in his sleep. The caretaker is leaning forward shaking his head as if to say, "No matter how many times I hear it..." I look out at the encroaching darkness and think of that long drive home we must now make. The gentleman says, "Well, that's the story of that ghost, and I think it is our best-authenticated and most remarkable one." This does not make us feel any better. Perhaps seeing our distress, he then offers to tell us a somewhat more humorous tale before sending us on our way.

A good friend of his was over one summer night (some time before the granddaughter and her friend had made their visit) and, as was their custom, they went down to the river for a midnight swim. After their swim, they were standing on the shore when his friend said, "Holy... what's that?" pointing out at the water. "There's something sitting on that log out there." The gentleman could not see it from where he was standing and so moved down toward his friend, just in time to see something fading away. They waited a minute or two and suddenly saw a glow, and then the shape appeared again. It looked very much like a woman with long hair, sitting on a log in the river. "Well, I had told my friend the story, but he was absolutely cynical and had never believed me – but now he was convinced." They debated briefly about what they should do. Perhaps they should swim out? No, they decided, take the boat instead. It was only at that moment, as they were moving toward the boat, that they realized they were not dressed to meet a ghost, "In fact, we were not dressed at all! And, well, we thought we'd be at a bit of a disadvantage. So, there was no further pursuit on that one."

Jeff and I do laugh, a little, but I've a feeling it is more out of discomfort than anything. Somehow this story did not help shake the cold feeling we both have, like chilled fingers were walking down our spines.

"We are not asking anyone else to believe these stories. I would only repeat that we have been rigorous in our investigation. When we have accepted a story as authentic, there has been good cause — at least two witnesses, or experienced by those who hadn't known the stories before." Finally he strikes a match and works at lighting his pipe. He leans forward and says, "The only thing we can do is relax and enjoy it. Our attitude has been one of being open to things we don't understand. There is a hell of a lot we don't understand. And there may always be that frontier we can't cross. I think we're wiser people to accept that there is, and be grateful for the little glimpses we see beyond the frontier of present knowledge."

We turn off the camera and tape recorder and pack up. We thank him and make our way out to the car. Jeff says, "He is an intelligent, trustworthy, sane individual. He's a member of the Order of Canada, you know, worked for Parliament — how can I not believe?" And I agree with him. How can we not believe? We climb into the car and make our way back up the steep drive. Jeff turns off onto the little side road as I stare out into the gloomy darkness of the forest surrounding us, catching, every so often a glint of moonlight on water through the trees. "Uh, Jeff – please tell me you know how to get back home?" He glances at the fuel indicator, looks out at the road to the right and left and says, "Sure, it's this way....I think."

The Trouble with Haunted Houses

We are often asked on our tours why we do not visit more private homes or traditional haunted houses. There is certainly no shortage of such places in Ottawa. It is not at all unusual for us to be contacted by homeowners who are concerned about strange events or encounters in their home. We admit to being no experts on removing unwanted spirits, but we are always happy to learn more about our local ghost stories and haunted buildings. There are several good reasons why we do not normally include private homes on our tours. First of all, such stories often do not have as many witnesses or as much historical information to back them up as we would like. In addition, we also must be very careful to avoid upsetting the owners of haunted buildings on our tour, and since private homes can change hands quite frequently there is a greater risk that this could happen, especially if the owners' experiences are particularly terrifying. There are, of course, also some practical considerations. There are very few homeowners who would appreciate us telling stories on their doorstep every evening, much as they may love the Haunted Walk.

One of our favourite stories of a local haunted home took place in 1909, and was featured in the Ottawa Citizen in the 1920s. The home is no longer standing, but, according to these accounts, it was located on Augusta Street very close to Anglesea Square.

A lady from Renfrew was coming to Ottawa to visit some friends. During her visit, she stayed in the spare bedroom of their Augusta Street home.

In the middle of the night, she awakened quite suddenly to find that her bed was shaking terribly. At first, she was convinced it was an earthquake. She was quite terrified, but lay still in bed and waited for it to stop. After some time, the shaking stopped and she was able to calm her nerves enough to try to get back to sleep.

Just as she was drifting off, the shaking began again. This time, she could see by the moonlight that only the bed was shaking; other furniture in the room was completely still. She was paralyzed with fright and unable to do a thing but lie there in terror. After it was over, she tried to convince herself it was only a bad dream.

Before long, the bed began to shake a third time. This time, the sheets and blankets began to slip slowly off the end of the bed. She grabbed the end of her blanket and pulled as hard as she could, but a stronger force seemed to be struggling against her efforts. Inch by inch, the sheets and blankets were pulled from her grip and slid away to the foot of her bed. In a state of absolute terror, she jumped from her bed and turned on the newly installed electric light. When she searched the room she could clearly see that no one was there.

When she told her hostess what had happened, the woman was very surprised. Although they had only been living there six months, they had experienced strange events on several occasions. They had heard strange footsteps on the stairs, and heard a noise that sounded as though a large creature was crashing around in the attic. Unfortunately for the owners, they had a full-year lease on the home. They ended up leaving at the end of their lease with shattered nerves, as the problems got progressively worse.

Some of our haunted homes have troubles of a much more recent vintage. In the spring of 2003, we received a call from a new homeowner in Barrhaven, which is a suburb at the southwest edge of Ottawa. He and a friend had purchased a fairly new home for an excellent price, and were quite surprised to get such a good deal. The house was only about ten years old and located in a typical suburban neighbourhood. While renovating the house, the new owner noticed some very unusual things. He heard the sound of whispering voices coming from the radio, and naturally assumed this was some sort of signal interference. When he took a closer look, he realized that the radio was unplugged. The voices continued, and soon they could be heard coming out of every speaker in the house. This continued for some time, and then it abruptly stopped. A few days later, the homeowner was having breakfast in the kitchen when he heard a loud thump, like a snowball hitting the bay window in the front of the house. He went to investigate, only to hear a crash coming from the kitchen behind him. He turned to find that his chair had been knocked over and that every nail in the chair was pulled out. The nails were only loosely attached and were barely hanging on to the chair. The back door was locked and there was no one else in the house.

A few weeks later, he had some friends over and they left together early in the evening to go out for a few hours. He set the security alarms and the entire group left. When they returned later that night, they saw that every window in the house was now wide open. There were security bars on all the windows and the security alarm had not been tripped, so they did not think there could have been a break-in. When they searched the house, they discovered that a number of strange things had happened. One of the wooden rods supporting the banister on the stairs was completely shattered. They also found that every cupboard door in the house, upstairs and downstairs, was hanging open. Nothing was missing, but several glasses in the kitchen were neatly cracked right down the middle, and a brand new solid wooden chest in the living room was split completely in half.

At this point they decided to try to get help, and called us to see if there was anything we could suggest. We are certainly not "ghostbusters", but we suggested a few options and agreed to come and visit the house to see if we could find any explanation for some of these encounters. We called back the following week to find that their phone had been disconnected. Any further attempts to contact the homeowners went unanswered: they appear to have sold the house and moved on. Our investigation ended there, as our witnesses seem to have been scared off by the ghosts. One can not help but wonder how many great ghost stories are lost because the owners' best option may be to move on as quickly and quietly as possible.

Fairmont Château Laurier Hotel

Spirits of the Château

One of Ottawa's most recognizable and cherished landmarks is the Fairmont Château Laurier. The hotel was designed in the French Gothic Style of the chateaux of the Loire Valley in France, using smooth granite blocks and Indiana limestone for the exterior walls. Turreted roofs were covered in copper, which turns a soft green as it ages, matching the roofs of the Parliament buildings just across the Rideau Canal from the hotel.

Ever since the hotel opened in 1912, it has been one of the best places in Ottawa to watch the world go by. Debutantes were introduced to society, brides were photographed on the terraces, and state dinners have been held in the ballroom. Royalty, heads of state, and celebrities have all graced the Château with their presence, including Queen Elizabeth, Diana Princess of Wales, Winston Churchill, Dwight D. Eisenhower, the Rolling Stones, and John Lennon. Over the years, the hotel has not just been a place to spend the night, but an important part of Ottawa's social life.

While the hotel is a beloved part of Ottawa today, when it was being built, it generated a considerable amount of controversy. Local citizens believed that the hotel would destroy the natural beauty of Major's Hill Park, which is located directly behind the Château, overlooking the Ottawa River. Also of concern was the tunnel that connected the Château to the train station located across the street. It was believed that the tunnel was not only a health hazard, because of its lack of ventilation, but also because it would "attract pick-pockets, and worse still, gentlemen whose misdemeanors were of a far more serious nature."

Despite these concerns, construction continued and the hotel quickly gained a favourable reputation for its dignified hospitality. With its close proximity to Parliament Hill, the hotel became known as the "third chamber of Parliament", due to the number of politicians who often stayed and had meetings in the building. In fact, Prime Minister R.B. Bennett lived in a suite at the Château that had been designed especially for his use, at a cost of $98,000. When word spread that Bennett was only paying $400 a month for such luxurious accommodations during the height of the Depression, it made great fodder for his political opponents.

With such an important role in Canadian history, it should not be surprising to learn that the Château has some secrets of which few are aware. During the First and Second World Wars, the Château was used for secret meetings between military officials and powerful industrialists. In 1946, Robert McKeown wrote in the Montreal Standard "During the war, the Château Laurier was the scene of many a secret conference. Military and industrial leaders quietly entered the hotel by the tunnel from Ottawa's Union Station and went to work. Production and armament plans were laid behind closed and locked doors, while fellow guests passed by unaware down the thick-carpeted corridors."

Not all of the Château's secrets have taken place behind closed doors. On more than one occasion, individuals have committed suicide by throwing themselves from the upper floors of the building. Others have taken their own lives in various guest rooms: this includes one man who hanged himself. There have also been suspicious deaths in the Château's past, including that of a man whose wife was arrested, released, and then rearrested for the crime. Following a scandalous trial, the woman was acquitted, and the mystery of what happened in that room has never been solved.

Given the rich and sometimes dark history of the building, it may not be surprising to hear that strange and unusual events have been reported in the hotel. For over 68 years, the Canadian Broadcasting Corporation (CBC) had radio studios on the seventh floor of the hotel; many important broadcasts were made from these studios, including Prime Minister Mackenzie King's 1939 declaration of war against Germany. Many CBC employees have strange and unusual tales to share about their time at the Château. Perhaps the most intriguing is that of Patrick Watson, who was serving as chairman of the CBC when he stayed at the hotel.

Around one o'clock one morning, he awoke to what sounded like a pistol shot coming from within his room. Quickly sitting up in bed, Watson believed the sound had come from the middle of his room, where a table had been placed. Upon investigation, he found a heavy glass ashtray had cracked right down the middle. The following evening, Watson was awakened by a crashing sound coming from the bathroom. He discovered that his shaving kit, which he had safely secured behind the basin taps before retiring for the evening, was now lying on the floor at the opposite end of the room. These two events had a profound effect upon Watson, as he wrote in a letter to Château historian Joan Rankin; "Both of these events, trivial though they sound, were inexplicable and left me quite shaken. I will never forget them."

While Watson is one of the best-known guests to have had a strange encounter at the hotel, there are many other reports. Several years ago, two guests from South America were staying at the hotel. They were staying on different floors, one right above the other. One friend decided to take an old spiral staircase up to visit the other. As he began his ascent, he suddenly noticed he could hear a man's voice singing above him. Curious as to who was singing in the stairwell, he continued up the stairs. The voice grew closer and closer as he passed each floor and, just as he came around the last turn, the voice stopped. At the top of the stairs was a very heavy door that was closed and locked tight. The door was heavy enough that it would have made a noise if it had closed, and no one had passed him on the stairs. There was absolutely no other way out of the stairwell.

In the summer of 2000, we were contacted by a married couple who had stayed at the Château Laurier. The woman had several strange things happen to her while there, including the distinct feeling that someone had brushed up against her arm when no one else was in her room. The next night she was removing her makeup at a large mirror. As she watched in the reflection, the closet door behind her swung open by itself. Both she and her husband were somewhat frightened by these strange events, and by the following morning, she was absolutely convinced that their room was haunted. While having her shower that morning, she distinctly felt an unseen hand touch her right shoulder blade.

What makes these encounters especially strange is that both of these events happened on the same floor of the hotel. It is also on that very same floor that you would find the Charles Hays suite, which is named after the man who is believed by many to be the ghost in question. As the man who was responsible for

The Château Laurier Hotel in 1912.

Charles Melville Hays

building the hotel, and one with a tragic history, he certainly seems a good candidate.

Charles Melville Hays was born in the small town of Rock Island, Illinois on May 16th, 1856. From a very early age he was fascinated by the railway cars that would pass by his house. By the age of 17, he had his first job in the field, working for the Atlantic and Pacific Railroad. Hays quickly rose through the ranks, and in 1889, at the age of 33, was made president of Wabash Railroad.

In 1896, Hays was lured to Canada to assume the duties of the general manager of the Grand Trunk Railway. An aggressive, self-confident man, Hays was never afraid to push his own agenda for the railway. His ambitious nature occasionally caused him great trouble, as in 1910, when he adamantly refused to pay his employees at a rate on par with other railroad workers. A bitter strike followed, during which Hays hastily fired the strike leaders. When the dispute was finally resolved, Hays reneged on a promise to rehire all those he had fired.

Hays continued his rapid ascent in the company and in 1909 was made president of the entire Grand Trunk system. His vision was to create a transcontinental railway that was able to compete with the Canadian Pacific railway. He also wanted to build impressive train stations and luxury hotels in the major cities across the country to accommodate the travelling public. The first, and only, of these world-class hotels to be built by Hays was the Château Laurier.

In April of 1912, Hays was in London, England with his family, attending meetings at the Grand Trunk's head office. After the meetings, Hays had to return quickly to Canada to attend the grand opening of the Château Laurier on April 26th, 1912. He was invited by his friend, J. Bruce Ismay, President of White Star Steamships, to travel at a discounted rate on the maiden voyage of one of his brand new luxury steamships – the Titanic.

On that fateful night, Hays escorted his wife and daughter to a lifeboat, assuring them that it would take at least 10 hours for the ship to sink, plenty of time for a rescue. No one could have imagined that the massive vessel would be submerged in three hours. Ironically, hours before the ship hit the iceberg responsible for its sinking, Hays was overheard making the prediction that the race to build faster and larger ships would someday soon be "checked by some appalling disaster." A few days later, when the body of Charles Melville Hays was recovered, newspapers across Canada lamented his death as a national loss.

There is a very popular legend in Ottawa that furniture destined for the Château Laurier was on board the Titanic and went down with the ship. While it makes for a good story, there is no historical evidence to support it. Cargo manifests from the Titanic do not list anything as belonging to Hays or destined for the Château. Furthermore, as President of the railway, Hays would not have been responsible for purchasing or overseeing the transport of furniture. In addition, as the hotel was to open only a few days after Hays had returned, most of the furniture would already have been in place.

Hays had originally been scheduled to lead the grand opening of the hotel, but it was delayed in light of the tragedy, and the hotel opened with little ceremony on June 1st, 1912. Some feel that it may be the ghost of Charles Hays who haunts the hotel, and that he may have returned to the scene of one of his greatest accomplishments.

The Normal School, now a part of Ottawa City Hall

Spectres at School

Some of our most enthusiastic customers are children. Often, before a tour begins, a youngster will approach one of our tour guides to discuss possible explanations for ghost sightings and share his or her own unique encounters. Perhaps it is the innocence and naivety of childhood that allows children to see, experience, and feel things to which an adult mind may not be open. Many of the most chilling tales we have heard have happened to children, or involve the restless spirits of children long since gone.

There is no place with a higher concentration of young people than our schools. Given children's unique ability to observe that which adults may easily overlook or dismiss, whether as a result of overactive imaginations or an exceptional ability to perceive the world around them, schools and schoolyards are fertile ground for ghost stories.

Two of downtown Ottawa's oldest schools are located just down the street from one another. As you might imagine, the two schools had quite a fierce rivalry going, as bragging rights were always on the line. It also seems the two schools have something else in common. Both have resident ghosts that have been observed by a variety of witnesses, including students, visitors and staff.

Lisgar Collegiate Institute is one of Ottawa's better-known high schools. It was built in 1874, and was originally known as the Ottawa Collegiate Institute. Many important and influential people have passed through its halls over the years, including: Peter Jennings (television news anchor), Adrienne Clarkson (Governor General), James Naismith (inventor of basketball), Lorne Green (actor), Rich Little (impressionist), and Matthew Perry (actor).

In the 1960s and 70s, it was so well-known that there was a ghost on the top floor of the school that the students would only refer to the "Fourth Floor" in hushed tones and whispers. The fourth floor is actually above the top row of windows. It is a low, long attic that runs just under the roofline along the entire length of the building. The only window that looks into the attic is a small round one on the tower. The attic was originally used as a drill hall and rifle range for the student cadets. In the 1940s, the area was converted into a storage space, and was so used for many years. More recently, a new ventilation system has been installed, which has made it much more difficult to gain access to the attic. In the 1960s and 70s, however, it was relatively easy to sneak up into the attic. Students described the fourth floor as a dark and scary place filled with cobwebs, old uniforms, laboratory equipment and even a human skeleton from the biology lab. They would dare each other to sneak up there or even lock new students in the attic, hoping someone would catch a glimpse of the ghost. Some, however, came for another reason. We are told that at one time that it was possible to look from the attic directly into the girls' change-room, so that might be one explanation for why it was such a popular spot.

Most of the encounters in the attic were described as a feeling of being watched or the distinct feeling that someone else was in the room, even though the person experiencing this knew they were alone. Some former students have also seen a wispy form drifting across the floor. People on our tour have reported seeing a face looking down at them from the round window, and were quite shocked when we told them that it was the attic, which that was haunted. It can now only be accessed by the custodians and is kept locked.

Most of the students assume that the ghost is the spirit of Lord Lisgar, the man for whom the school is named. Lord Lisgar served as Canada's second Governor General from 1869-1872, and was known to be an independent thinker who was not shy about voicing his opinions. The students even joke that he's there watching over their football games and graduation ceremonies. It does, however seem a little unlikely that his spirit is responsible for the haunting. He never actually set foot in the building, and it wasn't even named after him until well after his death.

There are more probable, and chilling, explanations for the haunting. In 1935, a student at Lisgar was outside the building when a sheet of ice slid from the roof and landed on her; she died as a result of her injuries. After that incident, the roofline of the school was changed by attaching flat metal sheeting to stop the ice from sliding off. She could be haunting the school, keeping an eye from the roofline on her fellow students to make sure such a tragedy does not happen again.

We believe a more likely cause of the haunting may have to do with a custodian who spent a great deal of time in the attic. In the 1940s, he fell from the roof under mysterious circumstances. We have been told that he fell in full view of several classrooms filled with students. He was certainly killed in the fall. This particular custodian was responsible for converting the attic into a storage space, after the cadets were no longer using it, and so it may very well be his ghost who is haunting the space at Lisgar Collegiate today.

Just down the street from Lisgar is a heritage building which is now part of City Hall. Along with various meeting and conference rooms, it houses the mayor's office, which overlooks Elgin Street. When it was first built in 1875, it was known as the Normal School and it was the Teacher's College in Ottawa until the 1970s. It included a school where teachers could put into practice what they were learning. The front section of the building was where the student teachers took their courses, and further down a long wooden hallway was an area used as a "model school" where they taught real students in a real classroom setting.

In recent years, there have been numerous reports of strange happenings at night. The security guards have had so many different run-ins with the ghost in the building that they are now at the point of teasing each other about it. They like to hide their walkie-talkies around the building, and set them off to scare the rookie guards. They also had a life-sized cut-out of a woman dressed in old-fashioned clothing, that they would place in the doorways to scare other guards. But some of these guards have felt that such tricks could not explain what they have seen with their own eyes.

One of the security guards was not able to return to work, after his encounter with the ghost left him with debilitating nightmares. On one particular hot July night in 2001, near the end of his shift, he was doing his final rounds and had to make his way through the attic to check on the roof, as he had already done twice that evening. As he got to the attic, he felt as if something were not right. The attic was cold, despite the fact that it had only wooden walls sheltering it from the outside heat. He could not understand why it would be so cold. Suddenly, the room filled with a fog and a glowing figure appeared in front of him. It was a woman dressed in old-fashioned clothing. She told him in a soft but stern voice to "get back to class". He ran as fast as he could out of the attic and then out of the doors at the front of the building. He eventually quit his job, as he could not cope with the nightmares he was having after this encounter.

Another security guard who worked in the building in 1998 swore that he would never work at night again after he had a run-in with the ghost. He was working the night shift and was alone in the building. He noticed as he looked down the long hallway that runs the length of the old model school that there was a woman dressed in old-fashioned clothing coming out of one of the old classrooms. She crossed the hall and looked into the room directly opposite. The guard called out and asked who she was, and she turned and looked him right in the eye; then did an about-face and walked back into the room from which she had come. He took off after her, and when he entered the room, he found that she had completely disappeared. There were no other exits from the room, and he could not explain where she could have gone. He was shaken up, but even more so when he was getting ready to leave the building at the end of his shift. He happened to notice a display case in the lobby with some photographs from the old teacher's college. In one of the photos, he recognized the face of the woman that he had seen earlier that night.

The woman's name was Eliza Bolton. She was one of the earliest instructors at the teacher's college, and for a number of years was the only instructor supervising at the model school. She taught some of the first kindergarten teachers in Ontario from the

1880s until she retired in 1917.

There is a side note to this story. In the early days of the model school, each instructor would have been responsible for supervising two separate classrooms at a time. The supervisor would have spent most of his or her day walking back and forth between the two classrooms, which would have been directly across the hall from one another. After Miss Bolton retired, this practice was stopped and each instructor was given a single classroom to watch over. Perhaps Miss Bolton does not realize that she no longer needs to watch over both classrooms at once.

The Silver Bell
A Personal Account by Glen Shackleton

I think it is appropriate to end where my journey in ghost research first began. Although this story took place outside the Ottawa area, it was a very memorable experience that I have shared many times. In many ways it was this experience that first made me face up to the question of whether or not I believed in ghosts.

Many encounters with ghosts seem to happen during childhood. Whether it is because children are more open to supernatural experiences or due to some other cause is difficult to say. All I knew growing up was that nothing strange ever happened to me, something for which I was largely grateful. My older brother Craig, however, seemed to attract strange experiences all through his youth, one of which I managed to witness myself.

At the time we lived in an old eight-bedroom farmhouse in the country near Campbellford, Ontario. It was the sort of place where you would expect to meet a ghost on a cold October night, but was, rather disappointingly, inhabited only by the living. We had a large property and our grandparents lived very close by; only a field and a small creek separated their cozy little home from ours. Their little modern bungalow appeared to be the last place one would expect to encounter a ghost.

Our grandparents' house was a very popular hang-out. It was the place where cookies and sugary drinks were found in abundance, and there was always something entertaining for a group of kids to do. They had a huge television with an even bigger satellite dish on the front lawn (this was back in the days when a satellite dish was as big as a two-car garage). We frequently went there after school for video games and unlimited television, until we were forced to head home for dinner. It was a treasured experience, and the house was always a warm place for us to visit.

On one occasion, when a responsible person was needed to look after our grandparents' house while they were away, the decision was made to put my teenage brother in charge. He had been staying with our grandparents at their house for some time and it made sense for him to look after the place rather than leave it empty. He could come home whenever he pleased as we were only a short walk away.

I would often come over to visit after school and Craig would do his best to scare me by telling me stories about the place being haunted. Being a justifiably skeptical younger brother, I seldom believed him, but I had to admit that he seemed pretty sincere, and genuinely unnerved by some of the things that were happening in the house. He often felt the presence of someone in the house with him, and at night he would frequently dream of a native girl who would have conversations with him. On one occasion, she candidly told him that she was living there because her body was buried nearby.

There were other more physical signs of a haunting. The television would sometimes change channels all on its own, perhaps to something that was more acceptable to the ghost. When alone in the house for the night, he woke up to find that every light in the house had been turned on while he was sleeping. Most of all, he would find that objects would go missing from their usual place. He would search and search until finally in frustration he would ask the ghost to stop hiding whatever he was looking for. More often than not he would turn around to find the missing object sitting out in plain sight. It happened so often that he was firmly convinced that this was more than a simple case of forgetfulness. It seemed distinctly that whoever this was, they were trying very hard to get his attention.

Like many who have played host to a mischievous spirit, he really wasn't sure how he felt about these experiences. In his dreams, she certainly seemed friendly enough, and eager to make her presence known to him, but he had to admit that these encounters were often quite frightening.

I had heard these stories many times before but wasn't entirely sure what to make of them. Like most people, I had a healthy fear of such things but wasn't convinced that this wasn't just the product of an overactive imagination. In either case, it didn't dissuade me from the opportunity to spend many an evening with no adult supervision, playing video games and hanging out with my brother.

We spent some time watching television and eating junk food before heading off for a round of "Impossible Mission" on the Commodore 64, neglecting, of course, to turn off the television or tidy up after ourselves. After playing long enough to develop "joystick thumb", we went to the kitchen and fixed ourselves a snack. As we made up some sandwiches, we got to discussing some of our grandmother's eccentricities. Our grandmother was a lovely lady who relished the role of spoiling her grandchildren as much as they could possibly stand. She would always make an effort to gather together anything that she thought would make her grandchildren happy. Most of the time she got it absolutely right, but sometimes her ideas of what young boys would enjoy were a little off the mark. In particular, we were discussing her collection of musical ornaments. By musical ornaments I am not referring to fancy music boxes or the kind of thing you might find in a store these days. These were early plastic electronic decorations that looked somewhat cheap and often sounded much worse. The collection ranged from little birdhouses to Christmas ornaments to miniature pianos, but they all played electronic music or sound effects. We both agreed that the "Silver Bell" was the worst of the lot. This was a round silvery ball with a red ribbon for hanging on the Christmas tree. It was a little rusty and had a switch that was very difficult to turn on or off. When you did turn it on, you were treated to an unpleasant medley of electronic-sounding and vaguely creepy Christmas carols, like an old record player that kept changing speeds.

We had a bit of a chuckle and then decided to find the silver bell and have a listen. Our grandmother always kept these ornaments in the same place – together in a box on an end table that stored various books and toys. We had a look through the box, but the silver bell was nowhere to be found. A little surprised that it was missing, we spent several minutes turning the living room upside down trying to find it, before realizing we were wasting valuable time and returning to our video games.

Around an hour later, it was my brother's turn on the computer and I was dutifully watching the game in progress when I distinctly heard a familiar sound. Over the sound of the game and the television in the background I could hear a slowed-down and particularly spooky electronic version of "Jingle Bells" playing in the other room. Craig clearly seemed to have heard it as well, but kept right on playing his game. I grabbed his arm and quietly asked "Is that what I think it is?" He replied with a vehement "Shut up! That's not what it is!" It dawned on me very quickly that he was completely freaking out. He was refusing to believe it, end of story. I turned down the volume on the game and insisted that I could hear the silver bell playing in the other room. We turned and looked at each other and I repeated my question. I could see it written all over his face that he was definitely hearing the music, but he denied it again, this time shouting a curt "No!" At that moment, the music stopped. We got up and slowly crept out to the living room where we found the silver bell, sitting silently in the centre of the table. Craig picked it up and showed me that it was turned off. With some effort he turned it on and the music started up again. He turned to me and with a look on his face like I should know what he was really thinking he nervously said "Heh...maybe we should take this bell home to mom? I think she might like to see it." We both walked very slowly and purposefully out the door, making great efforts to look calm and unconcerned. We put on our coats and boots, went out the front door, and ran like hell all the way home. To add to the indignity of the situation, in the darkness I managed to miss the little bridge across the creek and fell in up to my knees. We did not stop running until we made it safely home.

My mother's reaction was predictable and certainly understandable. She chastised me for falling for one of my brother's pranks (though he was equally terrified), and told us that we would have to go back in the morning to clean the place up. Craig got called away in the morning to cut a neighbour's lawn and the duty of tidying up fell to me. Never has a cleaning job been done so quickly and with so many frightened tears.

Appendix A:
A Brief History of Ottawa

Who would have thought that the meeting point of the Ottawa River, the Rideau River and the Gatineau River would someday become the beautiful capital we know today as Ottawa? It was not a random decision, to establish a city at the convergence of three rivers. Even before the first French colonists arrived, the local native peoples often used the connecting rivers for their commercial trade. In 1613, Champlain came to explore the region, drew the first maps of the area, and even lost his astrolabe, which was not unearthed until 254 years later. When Montreal was founded, the Ottawa River played important roles in both the fur trade and the exploration of the continent's interior. However, the region remained a largely transitory place, as the rough climate, the swamps and the rocky soil discouraged possible settlers. The region would have to wait until 1800 for a permanent settlement to be established.

Philemon Wright, who came from Massachussetts, settled with his family on the northern shore of the Ottawa River, with five other families and 25 laborers, where the city of Gatineau (Hull sector) is now. His dream was to start a utopian farming community. He was also responsible for starting the lumber industry in the region, the main staple of the local economy that would guarantee the region's survival over the years. By 1812, the little village of Wrightstown had 1000 inhabitants, and a few families had started building their homes on the southern shore of the river, where the future city of Ottawa would stand. At the end of the War of 1812, there was the first wave of settlement on the southern shore of the Ottawa River. British soldiers were encouraged to settle in Upper Canada. In particular, many Highland Scots took the offer.

The War of 1812 also helped British authorities realize the vulnerability of the St. Lawrence River to American attack. The river linked two cities vital to the colony: Montréal and Kingston. Montréal was the commercial and military warehouse of the British colonies, while Kingston, with Fort Henry, was the fortress protecting Upper Canada from invasions from the south. The only direct transportation link between the two cities was the St. Lawrence River. This was a slow and expensive mode of transportation. If the Americans ever attacked again, they could easily control the main supply route by taking control of the river. This would severely paralyze the whole colony, and Kingston would be isolated. A new route had to be built. All eyes were turned to the Rideau River. By linking all the lakes and water systems of the Rideau River and the Ottawa River, a route could be made from Kingston to Montréal without having to use the St. Lawrence.

The engineer chosen to take on the important project was Lieutenant Colonel John By. The construction started in the fall of 1826. This was the most ambitious engineering project in the entire British Empire, and it attracted a variety of workers who eventually settled in the area. By 1827, French-Canadian lumberjacks, Irish labourers and British merchants and landowners had all come together to form the diverse foundation of this small bustling village, which became known as Bytown.

The construction of the Rideau Canal's 202 kilometers

linking Kingston to Ottawa was completed in 1832. The work was difficult, dangerous and done almost entirely by hand. The work days were long, from 14 to 16 hours, and the pay was very low. The majority of workers were poor and Irish, and many lost their lives on the job.

As there were no official records kept, the estimated number of laborers who died during the construction ranges from 500 to 1,000, with thousands more being injured or maimed in the process. The daily dangers these men faced included being smothered by falling trees and stones, being caught in blast explosions, and falling ill from the rampant diseases that swept through the workforce. The worst of these diseases was "swamp fever", more commonly known as malaria, which killed hundreds of labourers.

During the construction of the canal, the little village of Bytown grew into two distinct communities, divided not only by geography but also by race, religion and wealth. Upper Town, the neighborhood west of the Canal on the high ground, was colonized predominantly by English-speaking Protestants. The genteel British society that settled in Upper Town had the support of the local farmers, who looked to them for social and political leadership. They had a common antipathy toward the merchants and raftsmen who lived in Lower Town.

Lower Town was located east of the Canal and, at first, was an impenetrable swamp. In the spring of 1827, Colonel By started to drain the swamp and the land quickly improved. The best properties were given to Colonel By's friends and the rest was leased to Catholic laborers, namely the French-Canadians and Irish. Merchants and tavern-keepers who wanted to take advantage of the working-class clientele also settled their businesses in Lower Town. To the south, along the Canal, Colonel By gave permission to the poorer Irish workers, squatters, to set up their log shanties in a neighbourhood known as Corkstown.

Bytown was French and English, Catholic and Protestant, made up of lumberjacks, labourers, merchants, landowners, bureaucrats, conservatives and liberals. Each group had their own economic role, their own territory, their own religion, their own claims and demands, and they were all very reluctant to make any concessions to the others. These differences caused a lot of friction. Bytown was known in those early days as a dangerous, rough-and-tumble town, where violence was commonplace.

In Lower Town, the French-Canadians and the Irish were competing for the same jobs. This rivalry quickly became a source of major conflicts. Street fights, riots, and brawls would periodically break out. By 1835, the Irish had rallied behind a leader, and had started a campaign to drive out the French. The Shiners, an Irish gang, terrorized the population of Bytown: they attacked the French-speaking citizens at random in the streets, they set fires, they poisoned wells, they stole, and they murdered. The Shiners also started to intimidate the genteel society living in Upper Town. In 1837-1838, the army had to step in to put an end to the troubles. The conflicts between the different ethnic groups would usually calm down during prosperous years, and flare up quickly in difficult times.

Even in days of celebration, Bytown residents were sometimes so rowdy that it is easy to see how it earned its rough reputation. The first fair in Bytown was held in July of 1829, and it was such a terrible and chaotic affair that many years went by before another was allowed to be held in the town. The disastrous event took place at the corner of Wellington and Kent, just near the spot where the Supreme Court now stands. Tents were set up, and the whisky flowed like water for the fairgoers, while fiddlers and pipers played for the crowd. A horse race was the feature of the day, and betting was furious. In the end, the race was so evenly matched that even the judges could not decide who had been the winner. Bettors who wanted to collect their winnings grew furious as they waited, and a battle erupted in the street. Fists flew and the brawl quickly overwhelmed the entire fairground. Three hours later, those who were still able to stand were dragging themselves home. The participants could be easily identified for the next few days because of their black eyes and bandages. This type of rowdy behaviour would be typical in the years that followed in Bytown.

After the construction of the Canal, the lumber industry gave a kick-start to the local economy, but industrial development was still fairly slow. In 1840, Bytown only had one sawmill, one shingle mill, one distillery, one tannery, three breweries and two foundries. It was a small development built entirely on local demand. Merchants, craftsmen and professionals also settled in Bytown: bootmakers, bakers, harness-makers, doctors, and lawyers. However, Bytown's main economic purpose was to offer services to the raftsmen passing through. These travellers spent most of their leisure time and money in Lower Town, in the many taverns and brothels.

The streets of Bytown were filled with dust in the summertime, frozen in the winter and muddy in the spring. Sidewalks were made from wooden planks that were frequently missing or stolen. There were no sewers, and public services were too few to mention in a city that was small and overcrowded.

In the 1840s, Bytown was a prosperous little city that was starting to organize itself. A municipal government was put in place to take care of the sewer system, the drinking water supply, the maintenance of streets and sidewalks, the fire services, the rules and regulations on taverns, and prices and quality norms. In 1846, petitions were sent to the provincial government to ask that a police force be introduced to control the many outbursts of violence, but the city would have to wait until 1862 before a county jail was built to manage the unruly citizens.

Without a proper police force, in a town that continued to be very much divided both religiously and politically, Bytown had more than its fair share of riots and battles in the streets. The worst of these were the Stony Monday Riots of 1849. They were also the last in a long history of riots in Ottawa.

The riots started over a proposed visit by the Governor General, Lord Elgin, who was considering Ottawa as a possible location for the new capital. The mostly French and Irish Reformers, now what we call Liberals, supported Lord Elgin while the English conservative Tories were incensed over some recent political decisions he had made. The Tory mayor refused to hold a vote in council to invite Lord Elgin to speak, so two opposing city councillors called their own meeting of supporters for Monday, September 17th, 1849, to pass a motion to invite the Governor General on their own. Upon hearing this, the mayor scheduled his own meeting for the Wednesday, to pass the opposite motion.

Tensions ran high that Monday as both groups gathered for the first meeting in Lower Town, with more than a thousand people present. When the two sides met on York Street, almost immediately the pushing and shoving began and punches were thrown. Moments later, a stone flew through the air, followed by dozens, and then hundreds more. A full-scale battle erupted, with a regular hail of stones falling from above, and several pistol shots ringing out from the mob. It ended when the mayor led a unit of the local militia into the midst of the opposing crowd and arrested every Reformer in sight. Not a single supporter of the mayor was arrested that day, and when it was over, there was one man dead and thirty wounded.

As nothing had been resolved, both sides prepared for the scheduled rematch on the Wednesday, adding additional weaponry and manpower. The Reformers numbered 1,100 men, and had got their hands on three small cannons, sixty rifles with bayonets and close to 300 other firearms that had been taken from the militia armory in Hull. Across the Sapper's Bridge in Upper Town were 1,700 supporters of the mayor, armed with more than a thousand firearms and nine cannon. The British Ordnance, the unfortunate soldiers who had the duty of protecting and maintaining the canal, numbered only fifty men and put themselves directly in between the two groups on the Sapper's Bridge. They politely informed the leaders of each mob that an artillery detachment stationed on Barrack's Hill, where the Parliament Buildings now stand, had several large guns trained on the two crowds. They would open fire if they heard any shots from either side. It did not take long for the leaders to realize that they would be better off to disperse the crowds peacefully at that point, and the battle was thus prevented. Needless to say, the Governor General called off his visit, and could not be convinced to return until 1854, after which Ottawa was finally made the capital of Canada. Bytown became incorporated as the city of Ottawa in 1855.

Given the events of the past, one can understand why some people thought that Ottawa might not be a shining choice as the new capital of the country. There was even a popular rumour that Queen Victoria had chosen Ottawa in a game of pin the tail on the donkey, in which she was blindfolded and stuck a pin randomly into a map of Canada. One writer of the time was quoted as saying that the choice of Ottawa as capital made it a "sub-arctic timber village transformed by royal mandate into a political cockpit". All the same, it does seem that there were several good reasons behind the choice. Strategically, Ottawa was safer as it was farther away from the American border than many other potential sites. Ottawa also had a very diverse population – evenly divided among the French, the English, the Irish, and the Scots, which represented the diverse population of the entire colony at the time. The city was on the border of the two main provinces, and there was plenty of room to build the Parliament Buildings and to grow as a capital. Other cities that were also considered were Kingston, Toronto, Montréal and Québec City, but in the end, Ottawa was chosen as the capital in 1857, ten years before Confederation.

Today, Ottawa is still the seat of government in Canada, playing a role in the major decisions that shape the nation. Its world-renowned museums and cultural institutions attract visitors from across the country and around the globe. Its festivals and celebrations, including the spectacular Canada Day celebration on Parliament Hill, capture the complexity and uniqueness of what it means to be Canadian. Even today, if one listens carefully for whispers from the past, there is still the influence of that small and troubled timber village, where times were often difficult, but the dreams of something better were never extinguished.

Bibliography

Bond, Courtney C.J., City on the Ottawa, Ottawa: National Capital Commission, 1967.

Brault, Lucien, Ottawa Old & New, Ottawa: Ottawa Historical Information Institute, 1946.

Corbin, Lucy G., Ottawa: A Guide to Heritage Structures, Ottawa: Local Architectural Conservation Advisory Committee, City of Ottawa, 2000.

Craske, Peter, Law and Order in the Early Days of Bytown/Ottawa, Ottawa: The Historical Society of Ottawa, 1992.

Esberey, Joy E., Knight of the Holy Spirit: A study of William Lyon MacKenzie King, Toronto: University of Toronto Press, 1980.

Finnegan, Joan, Lisgar Collegiate Institute: 1843 - 1993, Ottawa: Lisgar Alumni Association, 1993.

Gwyn, Sandra, The Private Capital, Toronto: McClelland and Stewart, 1984.

Haig, Robert, Ottawa: City of the Big Ears, Ottawa: Haig and Haig, 1975.

Hirsch, R. Forbes, The Commissariat: Survivor of the Bytown Era, Ottawa: The Historical Society of Ottawa, 1982.

Leggett, Robert, Rideau Waterway, Toronto: University of Toronto Press, 1972.

Lett, W.P., Lett's Bytown, Ottawa: Bytown Museum, 1979.

Rankin, Joan, Meet me at the Château: A Legacy of Memory, Toronto: Natural Heritage Books, 1990.

Slattery, T.P., The Assassination of D'Arcy McGee, New York: Doubleday, 1968.

Slattery, T.P., "They Got To Find Mee Guilty Yet", New York: Doubleday, 1972.

Stacey, C.P., A Very Double Life: The Private World of Mackenzie King, Toronto: Macmillan of Canada, 1976.

Woods, Shirley E. Woods Jr., Ottawa: The Capital of Canada, Toronto: Doubleday, 1980.

Capital Case Files: 1932 - 1946 , National Archives of Canada.

Carleton County Jail Reports and Audits: 1943 – 1972, Ontario Provincial Archives.

Ottawa Jail Daily Count and Record Books: 1882 – 1887, Ontario Provincial Archives.

Newspapers

Bytown Gazette, Ottawa (Apr. – Sep. 1836)

Daily Citizen, Ottawa (Apr. 1868, 1875-1879,

Manotick Messenger, (31 May 1995, 29 May 1996)

Ottawa Citizen, Ottawa (24 Feb., 1995, 17 Mar. 2002)

"Haunted Ottawa" Series Ottawa Citizen, Ottawa (Summer 2001)

Ottawa Sun, (22 Apr. 2001,)

We also acknowledge the many people who agreed to be interviewed for this collection of ghost stories. We have not listed their names in the interests of their privacy, but we thank them for their many contributions.

As well, we owe a great debt to the many Archivists, Librarians, Historians and other researchers who were so generous with their time and advice. This book would not have been possible without their assistance.

Photo Credits

All Photos by <u>Katie Refling</u> except:

p.20   courtesy of the Bytown Museum

p.25   courtesy of the Bytown Museum

p.26   courtesy of the Bytown Museum

p.53   courtesy National Archives of Canada (C-017572)

p.54   courtesy Jim Dean, esq.

p.73   courtesy McCord Museum (M2003.145.6)

p.74   courtesy National Archives of Canada (Gordon H. Coster / C-075053)

p.78   courtesy National Archives of Canada (William James Topley / PA – 008467)

p.98   courtesy Josée Rivard

p.103   courtesy National Archives of Canada

p.104   courtesy McCord Museum (II-199189.0)

This book would not have been possible without the kind assistance of the many people who agreed to be interviewed.

If you have a story of your own to share, please write to us at:

Haunted Walks Inc.
P.O. Box 1218, Stn B
Ottawa, ON K1P 5R3
Canada

info@hauntedwalk.com

If you have enjoyed this collection of ghost stories, we invite you to join us on one of our world-famous walking tours.

For more information on our year-round haunted tours of Ottawa and Kingston, please visit our website at:

www.hauntedwalk.com

Also available:

Ghosts of Kingston
From the Files of the Haunted Walk

Printed in the USA
CPSIA information can be obtained
at www.ICGtesting.com
JSHW020928190424
61484JS00001B/5